TRUE
BELIEVER

TRUE
BELIEVER

Inside the Investigation and Capture
of Ana Montes, Cuba's Master Spy

SCOTT W. CARMICHAEL

Naval Institute Press
Annapolis, Maryland

Naval Institute Press
291 Wood Road
Annapolis, MD 21402

© 2007 by Scott W. Carmichael

Library of Congress Cataloging-in-Publication Data

Carmichael, Scott W.
  True believer : Inside the Investigation and capture of Ana Montes, Cuba's master spy / by Scott Carmichael.
    p. cm.
  Includes index.
  ISBN-13: 978-1-59114-100-6 (alk. paper)
  ISBN-10: 1-59114-100-1 (alk. paper)
  1. Montes, Ana. 2. Spies—Cuba—Biography. 3. Espionage, Cuban—History—20th century. 4. Espionage, Cuban—History—21st century. 5. Carmichael, Scott W. 6. United States. Defense Intelligence Agency. I. Title.
UB271.C92M65 2007
327.127291073092—dc22
[B]   2006033369

Printed in the United States of America on acid-free paper

14 13 12 11 10 09 08 07   9 8 7 6 5 4 3 2

CONTENTS

PREFACE

MY NAME IS SCOTT W. CARMICHAEL. I work for the Defense Intelligence Agency (DIA) in Washington, D.C., and I am a mole hunter.

Mole hunters are spy catchers. More accurately, we are internal affairs specialists, like those employed by large police departments. We're employed by federal agencies on a full-time basis to identify and investigate the small number of employees who may betray the United States by providing its secrets to foreign powers.

In the professional parlance of my world, I'm a counterintelligence investigator. And as you might imagine, I am not the most popular guy in town—at least not within my own agency. But that's okay, because this isn't a popularity contest, after all. It's serious business. I often tell managers that if they see me coming their way, it's not because I'm bringing them *good* news.

To me, being a mole hunter is not just a job—it's a mission. If, like me, you have spent time in uniform, you understand the meaning of that term. It's the mission that truly counts, not the individual, and the mission that must be accomplished, for the good of all. To accomplish my mission at DIA, I weed out a handful of bad elements in an agency that is otherwise populated by committed professionals whose job is to provide intelligence support to grunt-level warfighters in uniform—literally a life-or-death proposition. At DIA we take that responsibility very seriously. Frankly, being "popular" or even "liked" was never part of the deal when I first set foot in the agency back in 1988.

Several years ago, I informed the Federal Bureau of Investigation (FBI) of a growing suspicion that one of our own DIA employees, Ana Belen Montes, was secretly an agent of the Cuban government. The evidence at first was weak, but I worked with the FBI over several years to develop the facts and finally bring her to justice. This book is the inside story of that long and ultimately successful spy hunt.

You may have read something about Ana Montes in the newspaper, or you may have heard a little about her on the evening news. But from what I can tell, those reports missed the significance of her case. You see, Ana Montes was arrested on September 21, 2001, just ten days after the September 11 terrorist attacks on the United States. Few news organizations—much less the American public—had much attention to spare for any other story. So it's not surprising that she faded from the public eye so quickly, if she ever registered at all. At best, her case came off as just another spy story.

But I know better. And now you, too, will learn the rest of the story. For the truth of the matter is that Ana Belen Montes was an extraordinary agent, certainly not "just another spy." The average spy case has far less impact on national security. Often it involves a small amount of less sensitive information, passed on during a short period—perhaps just once.

Ana Montes, by contrast, operated for sixteen years with impunity, becoming the U.S. government's top intelligence analyst on Cuba at the same time she was reporting to the Cuban government. She not only passed on U.S. secrets to Cuba but also helped influence what we thought we knew about Cuba.

Montes had no prior connection to Cuba; her parents were Puerto Rican, and her father was a U.S. Army officer. She was born on a U.S. Army base in Germany and spent her high school years in Towson, Maryland—a home-grown agent if ever there was one. Her case shows once and for all, if the fact required demonstrating, that Cuba has mounted a lasting, effective intelligence effort against the United States that we should pay considerably more attention to. I am confident that Cuba's efforts to penetrate the U.S. intelligence community at a high level didn't end with Ana Montes' arrest.

Who cares about Cuba? Just remember that Cuba has taken an active role (sometimes, a military role) around the world for many years, whether in Latin America, Africa, or elsewhere. Like any nation, it also shares intelligence with its allies, just as it's generally understood that the United States sometimes shares intelligence with Britain, Australia, and other allies. So when Cuba gets hold of our secrets—secrets that affect battlefield safety and the war on terrorism—Cuba's friends are likely to get the same information. And that's reason for concern, since Cuba has been aligned with such countries as Iran, Saddam Hussein's Iraq, Syria, the People's Republic of China, and North Korea.

As you'll see later on, at the time of her arrest, Ana Montes was within twenty-four hours of learning our detailed war plans for the post–September 11 invasion of Afghanistan. To say the least, I wouldn't want that kind of information entrusted to the government of Cuba and its allies, and I don't think the families of our service members then about to deploy to Afghanistan would have liked it either.

Or let me put it more simply: There's a reason secrets are classified. Our specialty at DIA is military intelligence. Sharing those secrets with a hostile power inevitably puts members of our armed forces at risk.

I harbor no personal animosity toward Ana Montes, even though I was part of the investigation that led to her arrest. I didn't know her well enough as a person to suffer from any sense of personal betrayal by her. We were not friends, and barely even acquaintances. Having said that, I do have feelings about her crime. I abhor what she did. I feel nothing toward Montes the person, but I detest her actions. Spying for another country may sound dashing and romantic, but it's not. And for a trusted government employee like Montes, it's a double betrayal. Even after all these years as a mole hunter, that's my reaction to any spy we discover within the DIA staff. Their betrayal sickens me, angers me, and saddens my heart. I'm glad that I played a role in catching her and putting an end to her activity. I just wish that it hadn't taken me so long to recognize her as a spy.

Some details concerning the Montes investigation are far too sensitive for public consumption. After all, members of the Cuban Intelligence Service are reading this book, too, and I am not about to reveal sensitive details of our investigation to them. I, on the other hand, am fair game.

I am fifty-five now, as I write these words. But I am just beginning to hit my stride as a counterintelligence investigator. I ride into work every morning with a smile on my face and a song in my heart. I feel, and sometimes act, like a kid of eighteen or twenty. But in terms of wisdom and experience, I am much more mature than that. In 1995, well before the Montes investigation, I received the National Intelligence Medal of Achievement for my work in counterintelligence, primarily for work in support of FBI investigations. I know what I am doing in this business, and I intend to become even better. My friends describe me as an absolute bulldog for determination and a maniac for focus on my mission. I believe they are right.

In writing this book, I've come to the task as a participant in these events, not an outside observer. I don't pretend to be a reporter or an academic; I didn't do additional library research or formal interviews. Instead, I've chosen to write about my own experience: what I did and what I know. It's the best way I can think of to bring you inside my world of counterintelligence and give you a front-row seat on the first major U.S. espionage case of the twenty-first century.

There are more spies operating in Washington today—of that, I am certain. Now, during a time of war, those spies and their activities quite literally threaten the lives of the brave young men and women in uniform whom we are sending in harm's way against terrorists and the regimes that support them. Fortunately, I am in a position to do something about it. And I can assure you I will strive to do so, every day.

TRUE
BELIEVER

1

AN AMERICAN HERO

FOR ME, THE ANA BELEN MONTES case began very simply. One day in April 1996 I got a phone call from a fellow Defense Intelligence Agency employee, Reg Brown. Reg is an analyst at DIA; at that time, he had been employed by the agency for seventeen years. He was a counterintelligence analyst specializing in Latin America, and Cuba was a country in which he had developed particular expertise.

The DIA is a big place, but as it happened, I already knew Reg personally. My wife Jennifer and I had known him for almost eight years. (Jennifer also works at DIA.) He's a genuinely caring and empathetic person, with a ready wit, a warm smile, and a very approachable manner. He's academically oriented and shares with his fellow analysts an interest in current events around the world. Like many analysts, Reg is also a bit shy and introverted, which might explain in part why he and I seem to get along so well—because I tend to be quite the opposite.

Analysts like Reg are at the very heart of the DIA. They are the experts who perform the agency's core mission of assessing the military capabilities and intentions of foreign powers. They create intelligence products upon which the senior leaders of our country rely to make decisions affecting the lives of our service men and women and the security of U.S. interests all over the world. As for the rest of the DIA employee population—security specialists like me, logistics personnel, and computer specialists, and so on—it's very simple. We exist to support the analysts.

Reg came to me in confidence with a concern about another DIA analyst. Her name, he said, was Ana Montes. When I say that he came to me in confidence, I mean to say that he was hesitant, despite our friendship, to share his concerns about Ana. Like most people, Reg wasn't eager to talk about one of his colleagues. It's a basic fact of the U.S. counterintelligence business that it's not easy for most Americans to point a finger of suspicion. We're conditioned from childhood against doing so. We don't tattle-tale. We don't snitch. We don't narc one another out. We don't even voice suspicions about another person without pretty solid evidence, because we don't want to get an innocent person in trouble with the law. And let's be honest. If you're wrong, sharing suspicions can also backfire. If others learn you've caused trouble for a co-worker, especially one who is innocent of any wrongdoing, they'll label you as untrustworthy. You might as well pack your bags and find yourself a new job on another planet.

So that's what I mean when I tell people that Reg is one of the true heroes of this story. We can't thank him enough. Because despite all that I just described, Reg still took a look in the mirror and did the right thing. He talked to me.

Reg had kept his concerns to himself until he attended a counterintelligence awareness briefing for DIA employees that month. The message sent to employees during those briefings was quite simple: Report your security and counterintelligence concerns to DIA's staff of professional investigators. They'll conduct a discreet investigation to establish the facts, and your name will be held in confidence.

With that final encouragement, Reg made his decision. He came forward and related his concerns to me. I promised to be discreet. Swore to it, actually, several times, before he finally, reluctantly confided in me. As he laid out the situation, it was clear that while he and Ana both worked on Cuban topics for the DIA, they weren't really co-workers. As a counterintelligence analyst, it was Reg's job to assess the effect that Cuban intelligence operations might have upon U.S. military operations. In the past, for example, Cuban and U.S. interests have crossed paths in Africa, where thousands of Cuban troops once served in Angola, and in Latin America. In the 1980s, Cuba provided military advisors to the Sandinista government of Nicaragua during its struggle against the Contra rebels. At about the same time, there were also rumors of Cuban support to the FLMN (Farabundo Martí Liberation Front) rebels in El Salvador. We can reasonably assume that wherever Cuban military forces may be found, Cuban intelligence officers may operate against U.S. interests. It was Reg's job to gauge the impact of those intelligence operations. Just a precaution.

Ana Montes, on the other hand, was by then the DIA's primary political and military analyst on Cuba, a position she had held since 1992. In other words, while Ana assessed the capability of Cuban military forces to interfere with U.S. military operations, Reg assessed the capability of Cuban intelligence to interfere with U.S. military operations. They performed similar, but not identical, duties. Both worked in the DIA's Defense Intelligence Analysis Center, or DIAC, based in a large, modular building on Bolling Air Force Base, outside Washington, D.C. You might think of it as a huge think tank. It consists of seven floors subdivided into thousands of work cubicles. Ana and Reg worked for entirely different directorates within the DIA management scheme. Ana was in the Directorate for Intelligence Production, generally known as DI, while Reg worked for the security office, which is responsible for both security and counterintelligence issues. Their cubicles were on different floors of the DIAC.

But they did cross paths professionally. Whenever Ana produced a written position paper on a Cuban issue for dissemination to the intelligence community and the Joint Chiefs of Staff (JCS), she circulated a draft of that paper ahead of time to several DIA offices, including the one in which Reg worked. Since Reg was the Cuba expert among the counterintelligence analysts, he routinely reviewed Ana's work before she shipped the product to the rest of the community. In the same way, Ana routinely reviewed Reg's work before it went into a final format for dissemination. The net result was that Reg and Ana were professionally familiar with each other, communicating occasionally on the telephone or via e-mail and sometimes seeing each other at meetings and conferences to discuss issues related to Cuba.

Reg had harbored concerns about Ana for some time. His concerns stemmed not from a single incident or observation but from an accumulation of small incidents and observations that troubled him in the aggregate. This is fairly typical in counterintelligence. Spies are very good at staying hidden—that's their job—and the first sign of an agent's activities is often a small one.

For example, Ana was one of several analysts from the intelligence and academic communities in the Washington area who occasionally met with Cuban faculty members from the University of Havana to discuss academic issues of mutual interest. There was certainly nothing wrong with that. In fact, attendance at such academic forums by analysts from any number of federal agencies was, and still is, a fairly common occurrence in Washington. Reg told me that Ana's attendance at those meetings was not suspicious in and of itself. But it still bothered him.

Reg also observed something else. Ana seemed unusually aggressive in her efforts to gain access to sensitive information, both inside and outside DIA. Now, what he noticed was pretty subtle. This wasn't a case of someone sneaking into a darkened building in the dead of night. She wasn't prying into safes or filching someone else's paperwork. Instead, he was talking about networking, attending meetings and conferences, and aggressively seeking participation in special projects. He told me that Ana had even wangled an invitation to an ad-hoc discussion of counterintelligence issues sponsored by another federal agency. If anyone from DIA should have attended that counterintelligence meeting (since it was an ad-hoc meeting, no one from DIA was actually *expected* to attend the meeting at all), it was Reg. Yet Reg hadn't even known that the meeting was taking place. Ana had essentially invited herself to participate in a discussion of counterintelligence issues that focused on Cuba.

While that may sound fairly minor—and more like office politics than espionage—the fact is that it was exceedingly bad form, at a minimum, for an analyst to cross professional lines that way. Ana's area of responsibility was Cuban political and military affairs, not counterintelligence. She made matters worse by failing to even mention the meeting to Reg, either before or after it occurred. It was almost as though she were hiding the fact of her interest in the meeting, and of her attendance at the meeting, from Reg. That, Reg felt, was suspicious.

So much for small clues and unusual behavior. The biggest part of Reg's report to me was potentially far more eye-opening. It involved a major international incident less than two months earlier—Cuba's decision to shoot down two private U.S. aircraft in international air space on February 24, 1996, killing all four of those aboard.

The planes were flown by members of a private organization called Brothers to the Rescue (BTTR), essentially a Cuban émigré group established to provide assistance to Cuban citizens who risked their lives while attempting to escape the island by sea. Too many unfortunates found themselves adrift, off course, and out of food, water, and fuel, far from the shores of the United States. Left to the elements, unknown numbers died. BTTR decided to lend a hand by patrolling the skies above those troubled waters. Its self-appointed mission was to spot vessels in trouble and then alert the U.S. Coast Guard to provide assistance as needed. Its members were truly Brothers to the Rescue.

But the organization had another function that was not related in any way to at-sea rescue operations. The Cuban government complained repeatedly that BTTR aircraft were violating Cuban airspace and dropping propaganda leaflets over Havana. The organization had a political as well as humanitarian agenda. The Cuban government called on the U.S. government and the state of Florida to curtail the organization's flights, but the flights continued. Finally, the Cuban government threatened to shoot the aircraft from the sky, if necessary, to stop the harassment.

Now, that was quite a threat. The BTTR aircraft were operated by U.S. citizens and others with permanent resident alien status. Shooting down a civilian aircraft is tantamount to murder. The murder of U.S. citizens is not something that a sovereign foreign nation should undertake lightly. And yet that was the course of action that Cuba said it would pursue.

On February 24, two Cuban MiG fighter jets armed with air-to-air missiles shot down two BTTR aircraft operated by three U.S. citizens and one permanent resident alien. The shootdowns occurred in international airspace, over international waters in the Straits of Florida, as the aircraft were headed for home. Cuba was in their rearview mirrors, so to speak. The aircraft had earlier violated Cuban airspace by flying over Havana without permission, but they posed no threat to Cuban security at the time of the shootdown. The bodies of pilots Armando Alejandre Jr., Carlos Costa, Mario de la Peña, and Pablo Morales were never recovered from the sea.

Reg Brown naturally took an intense interest in the story. U.S. forces under the control of the Defense Department's Southern Command (Southcom) began to scramble in response to the shootdown—which was a Cuban military action, after all. It was Reg's job to assess the threat to Southcom forces posed by Cuban intelligence in the region. Reg was fully engaged. And the first thing he noticed was that the United States was losing the war of public opinion. Incredible as it seemed, the United States was being blamed for the shootdown. The Cubans had just murdered four people in cold blood, and yet the heat was suddenly on the U.S. government to explain its failure to prevent the aircraft from taking off from U.S. soil in the first place.

The day after the shootdown, retired U.S. Navy admiral Eugene Carroll stated in a televised interview that he had personally warned members of the U.S. government that Cuba was threatening such a shootdown. The admiral related that he had recently traveled to Cuba, where he met with representatives of the Cuban armed forces. The Cubans had informed him of their frustration with BTTR overflights of the island and asked him what would happen if they shot down BTTR aircraft. Admiral Carroll said that he told them it would be a public relations disaster. Upon his return to the United States, he said, he met with U.S. government officials and warned them a shootdown was bound to occur unless the government did something to curtail the BTTR flights. The officials, he said, told him they had been aware of such threats by Cuba for several months.

And just like that, the Cuban government found itself in a very favorable position in the battle for public opinion. The Cubans weren't viewed as the bad guys, after all; they were the victims. And the deaths of U.S. citizens were attributable to negligence by the government of the United States.

To Reg, the timing of these events seemed awfully convenient for the government of Cuba. Too convenient, perhaps. The Cubans had used their meeting with a former admiral to pass on a message to the U.S. government; he had met with U.S. government representatives on the day before the shootdown, February 23, 1996; the shootdown occurred on February 24; and, the next day, February 25, Admiral Carroll reported Cuba's recent threat in his televised interview. From there, it was an easy step for the world to blame the United States, deciding, in effect, that it was at fault. Reg wondered whether the short interval between the U.S. briefing and the shootdown had been planned ahead of time by Cuban intelligence in what's called an "influence operation"—essentially, a covert attempt to influence public opinion. He began to look into it. What he found, in the middle of that series of events, was Ana Montes.

First of all, he confirmed Admiral Carroll's report. The admiral did meet with representatives from the U.S. government on the day before the shootdown. Ana had arranged that meeting. As he had said on television, the admiral had led a team from his think tank, the Center for Defense Information, on a trip to Cuba in January 1996. Ana contacted him sometime after his return to the United States to request a meeting between the admiral and representatives of various federal agencies so that all could hear about his experience on the island. The admiral agreed, and the meeting took place on February 23.

The fact that it happened immediately before the shootdown was odd, and yet possibly coincidental. The fact is, analysts, academics, think-tank members, diplomats, lobbyists, socialites, and everybody—everybody—in Washington are forever mixing and meeting and discussing everything under the sun. This is Washington, D.C., after all. It is the center of the nation's political universe. Meeting and talking and sharing ideas and experiences is what people do here. (Some might even say the production of hot air is our biggest local industry.)

So it seemed merely odd to Reg, at the time, and suspiciously convenient for the Cubans, perhaps, that Ana had arranged the meeting with Admiral Carroll. But it was not sufficiently suspicious to prompt a report of the matter to me. Not immediately, anyway. Reg cogitated over it for several weeks, put it together with his previous worries, attended that counterintelligence awareness briefing, and then decided to lay it all on the table.

Reg's focus was on Ana's possible role in arranging the timing of events surrounding the shootdown (which, again, was nothing more than speculation and possibility). But he did note one additional item. It seemed a minor thing at the time, but still, it was rather odd. So Reg mentioned it to me—and it's a good thing he did.

Another analyst had told Reg about a strange incident involving Ana's behavior at the Pentagon just after the Brothers to the Rescue shootdown, and Reg passed on the story to me. Given her work as the DIA's military and political analyst of all things Cuban, Ana was, of course, called to the Pentagon after the shootdown to provide intelligence support. She was a key player. She was *the* senior intelligence expert on the Cuban military in the building that day. In fact, she was the senior intelligence expert on the Cuban military in the entire nation.

Now, in our military culture, some things are simply understood. I'm not sure how things work elsewhere, but I do understand how things work in the military. It goes something like this: If the chairman of the JCS or the secretary of defense, or their designated representatives, call you into the office because they deem your presence and participation necessary to the defense of the nation, then you simply go into the office and remain at your post, doing your job, until they consider your presence no longer necessary. That's it. No ifs, ands, or buts. Walking away at such a time just doesn't happen. It would be about as unlikely—and as noticeable—as a surgeon deciding to leave work in the middle of an operation.

Ana Montes understood that as well as anyone on the staff. She'd been employed by DIA for more than ten years when the shootdown occurred, so she was no rookie. At that critical time, the generals and admirals looked to her for answers to their most pressing questions. What had actually happened in the skies near Cuban airspace? They needed the facts, not speculation. What was the Cuban military preparing to do next? What were they *capable* of doing? How were they likely to respond to a variety of responses by the U.S. military to the shootdown? Ana was the woman with the answers.

Yet according to the analyst who talked to Reg, Ana left early. It happened after she received a personal phone call at the Pentagon. After the call, she announced not once, but twice, that she simply had to leave by 8:00 PM. And she did.

Before continuing the story, I should mention yet another unwritten rule at the Pentagon during times of crisis: You don't take personal phone calls. Ana stood within the very nerve center of the United States' military response system that day. She had no time, or she should have had no time, for personal business, however urgent.

Well, there was a serious disconnect here. Serious enough, anyway, for another analyst to have made a mental note of Ana's behavior and to have mentioned it to Reg Brown. The other analyst also said that Ana seemed very agitated by the call she took that day. No one overheard the conversation, but Ana's determination to leave the Pentagon by 8:00 PM was clearly related to it.

Reg Brown's read on the situation was this. If Ana was actually a Cuban agent, as he was beginning to suspect, then she was ideally placed within the Pentagon immediately after the shootdown. She would have known exactly what the U.S. military planned to do in response to the shootdown. But the flip side of the situation was that she was also trapped there, incommunicado, with no means of passing that information on to Cuba.

At the time, the Cubans would have been absolutely desperate for information about U.S. military plans and intentions in the wake of the shootdown. They would have been tearing their hair out to communicate with such a valuably placed agent, to learn whether the U.S. military planned to attack Cuba and, if so, when, where, and how. And so, Reg surmised, the Cubans simply called her at work, right there in the Pentagon, and instructed her to submit a report to them no later than 8:00 PM—which would have accounted for the deadline that Ana gave to her co-workers that day. Reg had quite an imagination.

That was pretty much the extent of Reg's story as he told it to me that day in April. In summary: a curious and possibly suspicious chain of events surrounding the February 24 shootdown of the BTTR aircraft by Cuban MiGs plus Ana's questionable early departure from her duties at the Pentagon after the shootdown in the wake of a personal phone call. That and Reg's gut-level feeling that something about Ana Montes was simply not right.

I had been a counterintelligence investigator at the DIA for almost eight years when Reg approached me with his concerns. I had never heard of Ana Montes prior to that point. She had never gotten into trouble of any kind, and concerns about her had never been raised to the DIA security office. She maintained a very low profile in the agency and appeared to be a model employee. But I found what he told me interesting and worthy of follow-up work.

I sensed that Reg's motives in telling me his story were pure. He had not related his tale in an effort to harm or defame his colleague. Instead, he seemed genuinely concerned about the possibility that she was serving as a Cuban agent of some kind, and he simply wanted someone to test his theory, come what may. The indicators of such service were thin and certainly subject to debate. But I had learned from hard experience that gut instinct has great value. I simply had to follow up Reg Brown's intuition.

Now, I work in the intelligence community. Under the law, I can go only so far in investigating a possible spy for the federal crime of espionage, and I certainly can't arrest one. In the United States, investigating and arresting criminal suspects, including possible spies, is the responsibility of law enforcement, not the intelligence services. In other words, it's the FBI's job. I felt there was enough information in Reg's story to take it to the FBI, and I did so. But I must say that they were not terribly impressed—not at first, anyway. I couldn't blame them. The reality was that there was simply nothing solid in Reg's account upon which they could build an investigation. So I planned to resolve Reg's concerns by interviewing Montes myself when time permitted.

In the meantime, a number of other cases competed for my attention. At the time, I was one of only two DIA employees who specialized in counterintelligence investigations. With a DIA employee population of seven thousand spread out all over the world, and with many of them in direct contact with foreign intelligence officers on a daily basis, I had a lot to keep me busy. In truth, I pretty well put Ana Montes on hold while working other cases.

About six months later, in October 1996, Reg Brown called me once again. The guy would not give up. During the summer of 1996 he had learned that Ana had been selected to represent DIA in a special Cuba-related joint project, along with representatives from other agencies in the intelligence community. Apparently, no one else from DIA had been considered for the project because, according to Reg, Ana had orchestrated the selection process to her advantage.

That bothered him. He knew it wasn't proof of wrongdoing. In fact, he realized that aggressiveness, competitiveness, curiosity, and enthusiasm are positive attributes in the analytical world. Reg realized that he stood on shaky ground by voicing additional concerns about Ana, but his instincts told him that something sinister lay behind her behavior.

After talking with Reg, I agreed to approach the FBI again. This time, although the new evidence was not much stronger, they agreed with me that the time had come for me to set up an interview. I began planning my interview—and my first encounter—with Ana Montes.

2

THE INTERVIEW

MY INTERVIEW WITH ANA MONTES took place on November 7, 1996, soon after Reg Brown contacted me for the second time about his concerns. In preparing for it, I reviewed the standard security file that DIA maintained on her. I noted a concern expressed by a co-worker at the Department of Justice (DOJ), someone who had worked with Ana more than a decade earlier, that Ana had voiced strong disagreement with the U.S. government's policy toward Cuba. I thought it interesting—and unusual for someone in Montes' position. In my line of work, such an anomaly is called a clue. I also noted that Ana had successfully completed a DIA-administered counterintelligence scope polygraph examination in 1994, just two years earlier. Her file was filled with accolades from previous supervisors and co-workers, and she exhibited no indicators of a troubled or disgruntled employee.

I decided to focus my interview of Ana on three issues: her role in arranging the debriefing of a retired U.S. Navy admiral just before the shootdown, the personal phone call she reportedly received while in the Pentagon after the shootdown, and her views regarding the U.S. government's policy toward Cuba. Everything else mentioned by Reg seemed easy to explain.

I called Ana a couple of days in advance to schedule the interview. She mistakenly supposed that I was simply updating her security clearance, a routine procedure that is conducted about every five years for federal government employees with high-level security clearances. I told her that I was not involved in her background investigation but that I had another issue about which I wished to speak with her. It would be just Ana and me, alone in the interview room.

Ana arrived a bit late for the interview, perhaps five minutes past the hour, and she immediately attempted to take control of the situation. She informed me that she had recently been appointed to the position of acting division chief, a job that encompassed many new duties, responsibilities, and demands upon her time. She hoped that our interview was not going to require too much time, because she had so many other things to do. She was very businesslike, polite, and pleasant. Masterfully done. In effect, she put me on notice that her time was valuable and that she wished to spend as little of her time with me as possible.

Well, no kidding.

Some of my friends tell me that I bear a striking resemblance to the late comic Chris Farley, the fat guy who appeared as a regular on the TV show *Saturday Night Live* some years ago. We look alike. Other friends compare me in appearance to the Pillsbury Doughboy for similar reasons. So I get poked in the tummy a lot. The fact of the matter is, I do not look like Louis Freeh or Edgar G. Robinson or James Bond, or any other ruggedly handsome G-man type. That's not me. I'm just a chunky, Joe-average white guy with a pleasantly round face. I'm not at all threatening in my appearance. I'm not intimidating. I seem to be easy.

But the reality is, I'm not a pushover who can be manipulated by chutzpah. Counterintelligence folks are not like that. We are a fairly independent, self-confident, and, generally, smug bunch. We are akin to submarine commanders in that we develop a rather skewed view of the world in the practice of our professions. Submarine commanders perceive only two types of vessels sailing the ocean blue: submarines and targets. In other words, they view themselves as something special—as hunters—while everybody else is just a target for the table. Counterintelligence guys have the same attitude. We're not intimidated or impressed by anyone. We have a mission to accomplish, and we don't care whether the target is a private or a general officer, a rowboat or an aircraft carrier, an analyst or a division chief. Targets are targets. In this particular case, Ana Montes happened to be the target. By attempting to maneuver out of my way, she simply heightened my interest in her. Bad move.

Although her behavior got my attention, that's not to say that I developed a deeper suspicion of her simply because she felt uncomfortable in my presence and wanted to minimize the time she spent with me in an interview. Not at all.

To a certain extent, everyone feels that way about submitting to an interview with a security or counterintelligence investigator. We factor that reaction into our evaluation process.

But her reaction did get me thinking, and the follow-on to it was interesting because it was not what I expected. Investigators deal with people a lot. The interview process is familiar territory for us. We learn to read people—not so much by what they say as by the nonverbal signals they involuntarily emit while under stress. We anticipate that people will react and respond in certain ways to what we say, at least in a general sense. Interpreting those nonverbal signals is not an exact science; it's an art. I must admit that I have no great skill in that particular art form compared to some of my counterintelligence colleagues, but even I can spot the obvious once in a while. Such was the case during the opening round of my interview with Ana Montes.

I'd dealt with this particular situation many, many times in the past. An interviewee enters the room and tries to seize control of an uncomfortable situation—in this case, by announcing that she was busy and short on time. Fine. The required response, on my part, is to regain control of the situation. In many cases, I can do so simply by acknowledging the comment, which makes the person feel more at ease, and then ignoring it. I get busy, I talk, I smile and establish rapport, then I ask some nonthreatening questions—and before you know it, the interviewee is so comfortable that he or she is actually happy to spend the needed time. Hey, I look like Chris Farley, so people should be happy to spend time with me. And that's how it usually works.

Sometimes, if the interviewee seems insistent on cutting the interview short, my response must be more direct and equally insistent. I'll say something like, "Look, I understand that you're very busy. But we have some business to conduct here, and we simply have to spend enough time to complete the interview process properly. Your security clearance is important. So let's just spend enough time to get this interview out of the way. It might take a while." Most people concede the point when I'm reasonable about it.

Ana wouldn't go for that. She was pleasant enough. But she made it clear that she was watching the clock. So I realized that I had to either cancel and reschedule the appointment or serve notice that she would simply have to take time for the interview as originally scheduled. Rescheduling was no option. It would have been tantamount to a concession that her time was more valuable than my own—that her business was more important than my business. Psychologically, she would have established a pecking order in which I was subservient to her. Nope. I couldn't have that. Not under the circumstances, anyway. I did not intend to engage in a debate or negotiation with her. She needed to understand that it was going to be either my way or the highway. So I suggested that she might be a spy.

Although I can't recall my exact words, I said something like this: "Ana, this is not a routine interview, and it has nothing to do with a background investigation. I do not conduct background investigations. I am a counterintelligence specialist here at DIA, and my job is to look for spies within DIA. Now, I've noticed some behavior on your part during the past year or so that suggests you might have been involved in a Cuban intelligence operation—a Cuban intelligence influence operation. And we're going to sit here and talk about that." Boom. Just like that.

It must have been a shock for her. I recall very vividly the stunned look upon her face. I heard not another word about her limited time or her busy schedule. Suddenly, she had all day to spend with me—which was my desired effect, of course. She eyed me like a hawk throughout the rest of the interview. I had more than her full attention. She was focused not only on my words but also my face, alert to every possible nonverbal cue. But I did not see fear or panic in her eyes.

Now, bear in mind that I did not honestly believe, at that time, that she was a spy. On the contrary, I had every reason to believe she was a loyal, true blue, all-American DIA analyst. Her employment references were impeccable. Previous employers absolutely loved her and sang her praises to DIA when she first applied for employment with us. Her performance during eleven years of employment with DIA had been beyond outstanding; she was a distinguished employee, a producer, and an award-winning, nose-to-the-grindstone, get-the-job-done type of person.

In eleven years, Ana had risen from the entry-level job of intelligence research specialist to acting division chief, a position of responsibility that very few employees could ever hope to reach during a twenty-year career. She had no financial problems and lived modestly enough to suggest that money and the things that it could buy were not motivating factors in her life. She'd committed no known security violations during eleven years of service, had been the focus of no security investigations, and appeared for all the world to have conducted her life in a low-key and responsible manner. And, of course, she had successfully completed that polygraph examination just two years earlier—the trump card.

All of those were pretty good indicators that Ana Montes was good to go and I was wasting both my time and hers with an interview that was based on little more than the well-intentioned gut feelings of one person who was not even a co-worker but just a professional colleague in occasional contact with her. I can assure you, from my own experience, that many counterintelligence specialists in federal government service would not have wasted their time on her at all, under the circumstances.

Fortunately, however, I'd been burned in the past, years earlier, when I failed to heed the gut-level feelings of a naval officer who sensed that there was simply something wrong with a fellow officer. Nothing else. Just a strong feeling that the other guy was not quite right. I was younger and less experienced then, so I'd blown it off—much to my embarrassment and dismay some time later, when I learned that that Navy officer's instinct was absolutely right on the money. Well, I'd learned my lesson, and I vowed at that time: never again. And that's why this interview was happening in the first place.

As I look back, though, Ana's response to my charge should have surprised me. I expected the shock, and I expected that she would stop trying to limit our time together. Those were my limited objectives in making my accusation in the first place. In hindsight, I now realize I should have expected to see and hear something else from her as well—disbelief and denial, even exasperation. And yet, she expressed none of that, or not at first. I should have realized that something was missing in her reaction—she was like the dog that didn't bark in a Sherlock Holmes story. But I missed it. I think now that I was so pleased with myself for having accomplished my goal of shocking her into submitting to the interview that I missed the obvious.

Think about it for a minute. If you were an innocent, hard-working, and loyal employee and some schmuck of an investigator who looked like Chris Farley or the Pillsbury Doughboy suddenly, inexplicably suggested that you were, in fact, a foreign agent spying against your country, how would you react? At a minimum, most people would say something like, "What? Excuse me? What did you say? Now just hold on there. You think I did what? I don't believe that I heard you correctly, buddy. You had better not have said what I think you just said. Why are you wasting my time with this? What do you mean by that?"

But she didn't say anything like that. She was simply stunned into silence. And I missed it.

What a klutz. I'd broken a cardinal rule of counterintelligence investigators. First, you must believe that the spy exists—that espionage is actually taking place. Without that baseline belief, you cannot expect to actually find a spy. You'll miss the clues, miss the indicators, and miss the vapor trails in the mist when you happen upon them. You have to be looking for the signs; otherwise, you'll fail to recognize them when you see them. An investigator should take note when the dog fails to bark. But I missed it. Sherlock Holmes, I'm not.

In retrospect, I should have known better than to enter into an interview, searching for answers to specific questions, without first putting my game face on—my skeptical, suspicious, show-me, prove-it-to-me attitude. I'd left it at home that day, apparently. And although I was following up on Reg's concerns, it seems I hadn't really, fully learned my lesson about listening to the gut feelings of others.

But if I missed that clue, I picked up some others. As the interview went on, I asked Ana to make a couple of lists for me. One was a list of people outside DIA she considered to be colleagues or close professional associates. The other was a list of people with whom she most often spent her off-duty time. My objective was twofold. First, I wanted to learn as much about her as possible. Second, I wanted to prepare the groundwork for my later questions about her conduct at the Pentagon after the Brothers to the Rescue shootdown, when Reg had heard that she received a personal phone call and left early.

One of the people on her lists was, it seemed to me, most likely on the other end of the line. By asking her to make the lists, I hoped to jog her memory, so she would be thinking about those people later on, when I asked her about the call. After writing their names on paper, it should have been easier for her to recall the phone conversation. Bear in mind that the shootdown occurred in February; our interview took place in November. Lots of water had flowed over the dam since February, and I expected her memory to be somewhat hazy. The lists would help.

Ana began to compile the lists of contacts. As she did so, she pointedly drew my attention to the name of a professional colleague who, she suspected, might be a Cuban agent. That was interesting. Her seemingly helpful remark suggested a classic attempt to distract an investigator's attention away from herself and onto another person. Guilty people do that a lot. Innocent people simply want to know why you suspect them of anything at all. At most, an innocent person will mention another suspect in passing. But Ana truly wished to incite my interest in the other person, and she offered to fill me in on all kinds of rumors. She was clearly trying to get me off on a tangent.

My alarm bells went off, but I feigned disinterest. I suggested that we might talk about the other person later, if we had extra time. But I wanted to address her issues first. And I made a mental note of her attempt to create a smokescreen.

I would get to my questions about the phone call in a moment, having laid the groundwork with the lists. But Reg's most interesting issue, from an investigative perspective, was Ana's role in arranging for the debriefing of Admiral Carroll to occur on February 23—one day before the shootdown. Ana needed to give me a satisfactory explanation for her role in setting the debriefing, especially the timing. She'd better not attempt another smokescreen.

Her answer to my question was perfect—absolutely perfect, and therefore disarming. It also had the ring of truth to it. The debriefing of the admiral had not been her idea at all. The son of another DIA employee had traveled to Cuba with the admiral in January 1996. He told his father about the trip, and the father, in turn, mentioned the trip to another DIA employee, who happened to know Ana professionally. That employee simply called Ana and alerted her to an opportunity to debrief someone who had recently traveled to Cuba. Debriefings of people like the admiral are quite common, so Ana agreed to do so. She called the admiral, they juggled their respective schedules until they found a date that was mutually convenient—February 23—and that was it. The bottom line was this: The debriefing hadn't been her idea at all. She certainly hadn't received instructions from Havana to interview the admiral.

Her answer took the wind right out of my sails. It so happens that I knew both of the DIA employees in this little tale. I'd worked with them for many years, and I could count on both of them to tell me the truth. If they corroborated Ana's story, then she was off the hook. To say the least, it would have been a stretch to suggest that Ana conspired with the Cubans and with two other DIA employees—both of whom had impeccable security records, including successful polygraph examinations—to debrief Admiral Carroll on a particular day, all as part of a Cuban intelligence influence operation. Nonsense. It appeared that Reg Brown's gut feeling and analytical observations had led me astray.

After the interview, I followed up Ana's story, and as I expected, the two other DIA employees readily corroborated her account. Reg Brown's best issue against her was kaput. It seemed that the debriefing of Admiral Carroll and the nearly immediate shootdown were merely coincidental after all.

Ana had provided satisfactory answers to questions about the admiral's debriefing, and I sensed that the rest of the interview was going to go smoothly. She was about to be absolved of any suspicion that she was working for the Cubans. I turned to the other issues on my agenda. There were just two more: Ana's personal phone call while working in the Pentagon right after the shootdown, which reportedly led to her early departure, and her disagreement with the U.S. policy toward Cuba.

Twenty-plus years of experience in dealing with people told me that she lied when I asked her about the phone call. I couldn't prove it, but I knew it. She claimed, flatly, that there had been no such call, no personal conversations on the telephone throughout that day. Not that she could recall, anyway.

I asked her the time she left the Pentagon that day, and she acknowledged leaving at about 8:00 PM. I asked whether that seemed early under the circumstances and whether others had left or were leaving around that same time. She recalled that she had been in the Pentagon since 6:00 AM and that it had been a long and stressful day, given the pressure under which she had been working as the senior intelligence expert advising the Joint Chiefs during a crisis. By 8:00 things had calmed down and she felt it was okay to leave. She couldn't recall whether anyone else left before then or whether anyone else was leaving at the same time. She denied telling anyone in advance that she had to leave by that time.

I then asked her to describe in detail her movements after leaving the Pentagon, and she provided a wealth of facts about her return home. Nine months had passed, and she remembered all those details. But she didn't remember making or taking a personal phone call, and she didn't remember telling people in advance that she intended to leave by 8:00 PM. We worked our way through her lists of colleagues and personal contacts to see if that changed her mind. Her final answer was no. There had been no such telephone call that day.

Bullshit. Forgive me for the use of questionable language to make my point, but I was the guy sitting in the room with her on November 7, 1996, and I know what I'm talking about. My assessment was that she lied to me.

The employee who said she had witnessed the telephone call and Ana's subsequent agitated behavior, who claimed to have heard Ana announce insistently, twice, her need to depart by 8:00 p.m. had no reason to lie, exaggerate, or fabricate that story. Hers was merely an observation, not an indictment of wrongdoing. She simply related the story to Reg Brown because her gut told her something fishy was happening before her eyes. The story seemed credible to me. It probably happened. Ana could have swept all of my doubts away by telling me who called. But she lied instead.

Looking back, I now understand why. Earlier in the interview, after she explained the role of other DIA employees in arranging the debriefing of Admiral Carroll, I made a point of telling Ana that I would check out her story in order to corroborate it. I told her very clearly that I would talk with the other DIA employees, since I could not simply take her word for it. Well, Ana had no problem with that. She understood my need to confirm the story. More important, she understood that I would go the extra mile to verify that she was telling the truth.

I believe that's why she lied to me about the telephone call in the Pentagon. She knew that I would check it out. If she told me that a person on one of her lists had called, or that anyone else had called, then I would talk to that person. Consequently, she could not simply toss out a name to me. She'd get caught in a lie. Her only option, then, was to deny that such a telephone call took place. And that meant she had to deny the fact that she announced, more than once, to her colleagues in the Pentagon that day that she intended to depart the Pentagon no later than 8:00 PM.

Ana was uncomfortable as she denied the story of the phone call. She was visibly nervous. But why would she lie about such an innocuous thing as a telephone call? Unless, of course, that call had come, incredibly, horrifically, from the Cubans.

Now I was on alert but confused. How was I to reconcile her innocent explanation about the admiral's debriefing, which later checked out as perfectly true, with the apparent lie about the telephone call? What was going on? Was it possible that the telephone call was truly personal—perhaps a lover insisting that she come to bed—and that she simply did not want to reveal something that personal to me? It was entirely possible. I remained open-minded (while reminding myself that she had, after all, successfully completed a polygraph examination just a couple of years earlier) but troubled.

Finally, I asked about her disagreement with the U.S. government's policy toward Cuba. Ana had acknowledged that opinion in two previous security interviews. I wanted to see whether she would provide a consistent answer to the same question.

Once again, she blew me out of the water simply by admitting her disagreement. She thought that the U.S. approach toward Cuba was in error. Like many other like-minded people, she had long believed that the U.S. government's approach toward Cuba was mistaken and counterproductive. She believed that if the United States wished to encourage the growth of democracy in Cuba, there were better ways to go about it than by confronting them, isolating them politically, containing them, blockading them, and preventing the free flow of trade. The policies and practices of the last four decades simply had not worked, and there must be a better way to get what we wanted out of the Cubans. Many people in government and academia also believed that the government's policy toward Cuba was mistaken. Some members of Congress thought so, too. Ana was very articulate and spoke with conviction. This issue was an emotional one for her.

Having said all that, Ana continued, she had learned long ago that some people mistake disagreement for disloyalty, so she no longer engaged in political discussions at the office. She said that she had never advocated the overthrow of the United States and that she had never done anything against the United States. It was true that she disagreed with U.S. policy toward Cuba, she said, but she was not disloyal.

Wow. She was good. Better than that, she was impressive—extremely sharp, quick, businesslike, mature, decisive, assertive, confident, and in control. Her answers to that question and to my other question about the scheduling of the admiral's debriefing were more than satisfactory. I could not make a case against her. As for the only other issue, the phone call and her departure from the Pentagon during the shootdown crisis, I had only my gut feeling that she lied to me. I didn't know why she had done so, but leaving work early was no crime. Now I had just two gut-level feelings to go on, Reg's and my own. She lied to me when the truth would have served just as well. Something was wrong.

As I mentioned earlier, I easily confirmed Ana's story about the debriefing of Admiral Carroll with the two DIA employees she had mentioned. Then I updated Reg on the results of my efforts. I could see that he was disappointed. He was genuinely worried that Ana the Spy, as he saw her, was going to slip away, scot-free.

Reg drew my attention to a flaw in Ana's story about how she scheduled the debriefing of Admiral Carroll. Reg couldn't let her completely off the hook on the issue of the timing, despite the fact that she did not initiate the debriefing idea. I might have dismissed his observation, but I understood that Reg is an analyst. He is trained to integrate little pieces of information into a whole picture that makes sense. As an expert on the Cuban Intelligence Service, he understood far better than I did the nuts and bolts of how that organization actually worked. So I listened to him.

Reg was interested in the delay of about three weeks between the time that Ana called the admiral in early February and the actual date of the debriefing on February 23. He surmised that she would have reported her activities to her Cuban handlers shortly before or after calling Admiral Carroll for an appointment. The delay before the debriefing would have given Havana plenty of time to put an influence operation together.

In Reg's scenario, Ana might not even have known anything about it. The Cubans could have suggested an approximate date, and she might have complied without knowing why the date had been selected. Reg thought that the Cubans might also have suggested that she raise the issue of overflights by Brothers to the Rescue aircraft during the debriefing. Next thing you know, the debriefing occurs, Cuba's reaction to the overflights is discussed, the shootdown takes place the next day, and the following day the admiral describes the advance warning on television. A public relations coup for Havana, and they get away with the murder of four people (three of them U.S. citizens) in international airspace. Perfect. But it was all a great stretch of the imagination and purely speculative.

The only arguments in favor of Reg's theory were these: It made some sense and it fit the facts. The alternative was to accept the very long shot that the timing of the debriefing of Admiral Carroll and the timing of the shootdown were purely coincidental, unrelated events. As a longtime investigator, I doubted that the timing was entirely coincidental. So once again, I stuck with Reg, and with my own growing feeling that something was wrong here.

My supervisors were not terribly impressed with my "case" against Ana. She was an outstanding employee with a spotless security record who had passed our polygraph just two years earlier. On top of that, her story about the debriefing of Admiral Carroll had checked out. I was dead in the water.

The FBI was not overly impressed, either. I provided a verbal back-brief to them and they accepted a copy of my written report, but they were not ready to jump on the Ana Montes bandwagon.

And that was that. There was no evidence to suggest that Ana was a spy—just Reg's intuition and my own belief that she lied to me about some telephone call, the nature of which was a mystery. We couldn't polygraph her based on that alone. And in retrospect, it seems unlikely that a polygraph would have established evidence of her involvement in espionage. After all, she beat our polygraph in 1994; we had no reason in 1996 to believe that another exam would have produced different results.

I closed my case on Ana Montes at the end of November 1996. I didn't forget her, but I couldn't justify the expenditure of additional time and resources to investigate an employee who appeared, on the surface, to be loyal and hardworking.

The results at the time may not have been as positive as Reg would have liked, but his report had planted a seed of doubt in my mind, as it should have. That seed germinated in my mind for nearly four years before finally taking root. It would reveal itself on the surface in a most unusual way.

3

THE MAKING OF A MOLE HUNTER

ALTHOUGH I DIDN'T REALIZE IT AT THE TIME, my interview with Ana Montes was the beginning of a truly major mole hunt, one that might fairly be called historic. In a way, I'd been preparing for it all of my life. I had cut my teeth in the intelligence business twenty-six years before that interview, while serving as an enlisted man in the U.S. Navy. After entering boot camp in San Diego in November 1969, I scored well enough on a foreign language aptitude test that the Navy sent me to study Mandarin Chinese at its language school in Monterey, California. The United States was embroiled in the Vietnam War at the time, and the Navy was naturally concerned about the security of its operations in the Tonkin Gulf, a part of the South China Sea to the east of North Vietnam.

A potential threat to those operations was posed not by the North Vietnamese but by the People's Republic of China, which maintained a large naval presence at the southern tip of Hainan Island in the gulf. The U.S. Navy feared that China might enter the war, so they employed linguists to keep an eye on Chinese naval operations just in case. I spent two and a half years in the Far East doing exactly that.

When I got out of the Navy, I took advantage of the GI Bill to attend college at the University of Washington in Seattle. My bachelor's degree was in East Asian studies, with an emphasis on China. But I had no real direction in my life, so I returned to my roots in Wisconsin after graduation. There I worked for my dad for a while in his machine shop.

I liked working for my dad. His shop was dirty, greasy, and unkempt—a guy's kind of place. I found it very gratifying to work with my hands, creating things of value from raw materials. Besides, it tickled me to think that I was almost certainly the only college-educated Chinese linguist in the metal-fabricating business. But after a year or so, I became restless. So I answered an ad in the paper and took a job as a cop.

I had never aspired to a career in law enforcement, but I liked the work, and I spent the next seven years of my life earning a living as a patrolman in the small Wisconsin town of Edgerton. I discovered I had a knack for working with people, which is what law enforcement is really all about. Just talking to folks, communicating. Occasionally, of course, it also calls for wrestling with a drunk in a bar or with an irate husband or wife during a domestic dispute. But mostly, police work is an exercise in the art of dealing with people under sometimes stressful situations. I found that I could do that and I enjoyed it.

I worked the night shifts for seven years and learned a lot about people from that experience. One thing I learned early on was that some people are simply wired differently than others, and I could never hope to understand them, much less to change them. The experiences in life that shaped their personalities and values were beyond me. I'll revisit that lesson later in the context of the Ana Montes case.

Over time, once again, I became restless. I was thirty-three years old, and while I was happy enough in my job as a cop, I was not satisfied with my accomplishments in life. I went back to work for the Navy in 1984, but this time as a civilian investigator for NIS, the Naval Investigative Service (later called the Naval Criminal Investigative Service, or NCIS). At first, I conducted criminal investigations for the Navy as an NIS special agent in the San Francisco Bay area. Then, in 1985, I switched to my current specialty, counterintelligence, and I've never looked back.

Counterintelligence is a specialized investigative and operational discipline aimed at countering the efforts of foreign intelligence agencies to acquire sensitive information about U.S. plans, capabilities, and intentions. That's a mouthful. But the concept is quite simple. Foreign intelligence officers reside and work in our country and around the world, and their job is to recruit Americans who are willing to provide U.S. secrets, whether for money or some other reason. It's our task in counterintelligence to detect, investigate, and neutralize their efforts.

I enjoyed my first experience in that line of work at NIS' office on Treasure Island in San Francisco Bay. I also met and married my wife Jennifer, who was also an NIS agent, while I was there. Based on my track record in San Francisco, NIS then offered me a tour of duty at its headquarters near Washington, D.C. Jennifer transferred to Washington at the same time.

Some agents might consider a tour of duty in Washington, especially at NIS headquarters, something to avoid. Headquarters seems so far removed from the action, and it's loaded with bureaucracy, oversight, and petty politics. But I felt lucky to work there, because exposure to a broad range of major issues at that level forced me to learn a lot about the business of counterintelligence. Lessons I learned at NIS headquarters came in very handy during the Ana Montes investigation.

In 1988, about a year after the birth of our first child, Jennifer and I were hired by the Defense Intelligence Agency. My job at DIA was to conduct counterintelligence investigations whenever the agency developed so much as a suspicion that one of its employees might be engaged in espionage.

It seems that very few Americans are familiar with DIA. The agency was established on October 1, 1961, about five months after the failed U.S.-backed Bay of Pigs invasion of Cuba. The Central Intelligence Agency (CIA) is often blamed for the Bay of Pigs fiasco. I don't know about that. I may work for the Department of Defense (DoD), but I do not claim to possess one scintilla of expertise in the art of war. So I can't pass judgment. (I'll have more to say later, though, about how the Bay of Pigs episode has affected Cuban intelligence priorities ever since.)

But I do know this: Congress had already been debating for several years the need to establish another intelligence agency, separate from the CIA, that would specialize in military intelligence. The individual armed forces already had their own intelligence services, as they do today. But there was no single agency drawing together military intelligence across the board. Policy makers called for an agency that would provide Pentagon decision makers with accurate information about the military capabilities and intentions of potential adversaries. The need was already recognized; at most, the public uproar over the Bay of Pigs served merely as the final catalyst for the creation of DIA.

In a sense, DIA serves as the Pentagon's scout. The agency surveys the lay of the land before the troops go in—long before hostilities break out, if they ever do. DIA analysts piece together potential adversaries' capabilities and intentions out of information that comes into the agency from a variety of sources—human agents, satellite imagery, intercepted foreign communications, and more.

Among other things, DIA seeks to determine an adversary's troop strength and weapons, where its forces are located, and where they are likely to be if hostilities commence. It needs to know how the enemy is likely to fight—strategy and tactics—and to identify its strengths and weaknesses. Far in advance of any actual hostilities, DIA locates, catalogues, and prioritizes every legitimate military target—every tank, plane, and ship; every bridge, power plant, and airport; every ammo dump and manufacturing facility—and puts them on a target list. When and if the day arrives, virtually anywhere in the world, when U.S. forces need to take out those targets, they can do so—quickly, efficiently, and with minimum risk to themselves. That's what DIA does for a living.

DIA also stays on top of political events around the world, and it tracks the movements of foreign military forces as they respond to world events. Wherever U.S. interests are threatened, DIA is prepared, at a moment's notice, to brief senior Defense Department decision makers with hard facts regarding the situation on the ground—including the size, composition, and capability of any foreign adversary with whom U.S. forces are likely to contend. In fact, that's what Ana Montes was doing at the Pentagon after the Brothers to the Rescue shootdown.

In a perfect world, DIA would maintain a complete library of current data on every potential adversary and every potential military target in the world. But resources and opportunities to collect information about foreign military forces are limited. So instead of maintaining a complete picture of our adversaries and their intentions, we are left with a mosaic—not quite a complete picture, but enough of a picture, in most cases, to understand the whole. That's where DIA's analysts come in. They are experts at mosaic reconstruction. Give them a piece of information here and a fragment of information there, and experienced analysts who truly know their stuff can fill the gaps with experience and logic.

About two years after I joined DIA, for example, Iraqi military forces moved up to the Kuwait border in July 1990. A debate quickly ensued among members of the U.S. intelligence community regarding Iraqi leader Saddam Hussein's true intentions. Many argued he was simply staging a show for effect and that Iraqi forces would withdraw in good order after making their point.

One DIA analyst, however—perhaps the only such analyst in the U.S. intelligence community—believed otherwise. He knew with near certainty that Saddam Hussein intended to invade Kuwait because he had studied the minutiae of Iraqi military operations for more than a decade. He knew from experience which preparations Saddam's military juggernaut always made before attacking opposing forces. He saw every one of those attack indicators emerge on the ground along the Kuwait border.

As a result, on the first day of the Iraqi invasion of Kuwait, that DIA analyst became a very popular guy within certain circles in Washington. First, he briefed the chairman of the Joint Chiefs of Staff, then the secretary of defense, and finally the president. Just as we did that day, DIA ultimately serves the warfighters, the policy makers, and the decision makers of the executive branch of government. They are our customers—the consumers of our intelligence product.

We are a proud and dedicated bunch at DIA. The agency's success over the years is self-evident to historians and analysts. Congress has been well pleased with our efforts, and the uniformed men and women of our military have been well served by their own intelligence agency. DIA's motto is "Committed to Excellence in Defense of the Nation." But it's more than a slogan. It's a credo.

There are several thousand DIA employees, including our core staff of analysts, at offices throughout the Washington metropolitan area. Other DIA employees are stationed at DIA offices all over the world, including the staffs of defense attaché offices attached to U.S. embassies in more than a hundred countries.

Defense attachés serve as military advisors to their ambassadors and as principal liaison officers to the host country's military forces. They also interpret military-related events in that country. A defense attaché is a bit like a foreign correspondent, except that the defense attaché is usually on the scene first and has the experience in military affairs to more accurately assess and report events.

In 1991, I had my first openly acknowledged success at DIA (we don't talk about everything that we do) when I identified a DIA employee at a U.S. embassy as a spy. His name was Frederick C. Hamilton.

Fred was a civilian employee at DIA's office in Lima, Peru. I'd never characterize him as a big fish in the espionage pond, but to me, the investigation was a great success—not only because I identified him and assisted in obtaining his confession, but because, at the time, my partner and I were virtually the only people on Earth who believed that espionage was even afoot in Lima, Peru.

(I had paired up with another counterintelligence investigator at DIA to work the case.)

We certainly had reason to believe that there was a leak of classified DIA reports from the U.S. embassy in Lima. Somehow, they were reaching the government of a neighboring and sometimes hostile country, Ecuador. But after a review of the situation, a seasoned FBI agent in Washington gave it as his opinion that the leak could be attributed to sloppy security practices at the embassy rather than an embedded spy. He speculated that a cleaning woman or another embassy worker had swept the reports into a bucket or that someone had inadvertently thrown the reports into the trash. Some Ecuadorian intelligence agent, completely unrelated to the embassy, was probably checking through the discarded waste and coming up with the reports that way. I spent the summer of 1991 trying to convince him otherwise.

I argued that the leak had to be deliberate. The specific materials that were reaching the government of Ecuador were of very high value, so the odds favored a leak by someone who knew those materials well. Many Americans on the embassy staff had access to the materials. But by discreetly gathering information and conducting analysis, I narrowed the list of suspects down to Fred Hamilton.

I failed to convince our seasoned FBI agent that my theory was more likely than his own. So my partner and I traveled to Lima to confront Fred with our suspicions. He confessed. We then turned Fred over to the FBI, and Fred was sentenced to serve a few years in federal prison for his trouble.

Despite that difference of opinion, I hasten to add, I've had a great working relationship with the FBI ever since. They are a pleasure to work with. Most of my work is performed with one particular squad at the FBI's Washington field office, but I've had opportunities over the years to work with many FBI agents throughout the country.

4

A SPY AMONG US

BY THE LATE 1990S, THE U.S. INTELLIGENCE community had had reason to believe for a number of years that a Cuban spy might be operating among us, perhaps in the very heart of the nation's capital. No one knew who the spy was or where the spy was employed. But it seemed obvious that a spy of some kind existed within the community.

Indications of a spy's presence were manifest. There was the CIA's persistent difficulty in running Cuban agents. It seemed that every operation was doubled back against the CIA by an incredibly effective Cuban Intelligence Service as agent after agent defeated CIA polygraph examinations. (Polygraph exams, conducted in mutually convenient locations, are common when working with recruited agents overseas.) Technical intelligence operations suffered as well, mysteriously drying up after short periods of exploitation by U.S. intelligence, as though the Cubans had been tipped to our methods.

Signs of the problem went back many years. During the 1980s and early 1990s, Cuba seemed to possess foreknowledge of U.S. military and intelligence operations in El Salvador, Nicaragua, and Panama. Taken together, these anomalous failures in our intelligence efforts begged for an explanation.

Some attributed the failures to the massive Soviet and Cuban (later, Russian and Cuban) signals intelligence collection effort at the Lourdes communication facility in Cuba. The Russians and Cubans were masters at intercepting and exploiting information carelessly divulged during telephone conversations

29

that were either originated by or placed to U.S. officials. For years, analysts and pundits alike cited Cuba's Lourdes installation as an easy explanation for the Cuban intelligence successes against the United States. Still, we couldn't rule out the possibility that one or more human spies worked among us, within the U.S. intelligence community, on behalf of the Cuban Intelligence Service.

For most of us in the intelligence community, Cuba's motives for such a penetration were a given. Earlier, I referred to the April 1961 Bay of Pigs invasion, an effort by the United States to overthrow the fledgling communist regime of Fidel Castro Ruiz. The proxy force of poorly trained and unsupported Cuban refugees was quickly defeated by the Cuban army at the Bay of Pigs. Thus was born, in blood, the modern era of Cuban-American relations.

There followed a series of covert attempts against the life of the Cuban leader that confirmed his belief that the United States would remain forever his mortal enemy. In October 1962, Castro and his ally, the Soviet Union, moved to level the playing field against the superpower to his north. With Castro's cooperation, the Soviets introduced nuclear missiles to the island in an effort to deter future U.S. attacks. The gambit worked. The missiles were removed, but only after tense negotiations produced an agreement that included a promise by the United States to never again invade the island of Cuba. Castro won.

Castro made clear in the decades that followed, however, that he did not believe the United States would hold to that promise. Right into the twenty-first century, he believed that the United States would one day again invade Cuba. Cuba's entire military strategy, its defense of the homeland, was grounded in that basic tenet. An entire generation of Cubans born in the four decades since the Bay of Pigs fiasco continued to believe that an invasion by U.S.-supported ground forces would one day occur again.

Castro also drew a more specific lesson from the Bay of Pigs operation. At first, the U.S.-backed invasion had some short-lived success in its attempt to overwhelm Cuban military forces and end communist rule of the island. The Cuban defenders were taken by surprise and unprepared to handle the initial assault. The invasion force originally drove Cuban defenders inland, as planned. Ultimately, of course, the weight of Cuban reinforcements and their determined counterattacks saved the Castro regime during three hectic days of fighting.

Castro vowed never again to allow the United States to catch him off guard with an attack. In the years that followed, he tried to eliminate the element of surprise by gathering information about U.S. plans, intentions, and capabilities. He needed intelligence. So he recruited spies.

Spies are relatively easy to recruit and to plant where needed. Anti-Castro Cuban émigré groups based in the Miami-Dade area of Florida were a prime target. In September 1998, the FBI's Miami field office arrested several of these spies and their handlers, collectively known as the Wasp network, in a round-up that effectively neutralized the Cuban effort against those groups. It made perfect sense that the U.S. government itself was also a Cuban intelligence target.

One tool used by counterintelligence investigators in their efforts to identify a possible Cuban agent was the development of a straw man. A straw man may be nothing more than a list of general characteristics—in this case, describing the type of individual who would most likely spy for Cuba. Such a straw man served as a template against which investigators might measure potential suspects to gauge the likelihood that a particular suspect was a Cuban agent.

A number of attributes are considered in developing a straw man. At the top of the list is an agent's gender. We had no hard information about gender, but it seemed likely to analysts that most Cuban spies were male. That deduction was based in part on the simple fact that the vast majority of Americans convicted of espionage during the modern era, about 93 percent of them, have been men. Of course, the possibility that an American spying for Cuba or for any other country might be a woman can never be entirely discounted, but the odds clearly favor males over females; 93 percent is a figure that cannot be ignored.

Next on the list of data points for a straw man is employment. Again, no solid information was available from which to work, but analysis of Cuban-related intelligence anomalies over the years suggested that a Cuban spy might be employed generally within the federal government and possibly within the U.S. intelligence community itself. The intelligence community includes a large number of agencies; given the integrated nature of the intelligence community today, a spy might find employment in any one of the agencies to gain access to virtually the same information. The spy could be anywhere.

It seemed likely, though, that a Cuban spy would be employed as a specialist in Latin American affairs. That was not necessarily the case, of course, but again the odds weighed in favor of a spy positioned to provide Castro the information he most urgently required: information about U.S. plans and intentions toward Cuba. No one could seriously discount the possibility that a Cuban spy might specialize in some other geographic region or in a particular discipline like counternarcotics, chemical and biological warfare, or counterterrorism. But it seemed a fair bet to some analysts, for the purpose of constructing a straw man, that Cuba preferred to recruit Latin America specialists.

That's about it. The Cuban spy among us, then, might be a man, might be employed within the intelligence community, and might be a Latin America specialist. Maybe. For that matter, there might be more than one of them. Unfortunately, this basic straw man was far too generic to be of practical use to a mole hunter. More specific information was needed to support our efforts. But such information was not easily obtained.

When investigators do obtain a few tidbits of information about a particular spy who is active among us, we too often hoard that information for security purposes rather than share it with our counterintelligence colleagues. That is a mistake.

And that is precisely what happened in the case of Ana Montes. A tidbit of information that might help identify a Cuban spy surfaced within the counterintelligence community. The tidbit was jealously guarded by investigators, both to ensure the security of its source and to prevent the spy from learning about their investigative efforts. I was not initially made privy to the information, and I had absolutely no idea that anyone was actively looking for a particular Cuban spy—until someone on the "inside" of the case violated security by leaking word about the investigation to one of my colleagues at DIA.

5

LEAKS AND MORE LEAKS

IN SEPTEMBER 2000, AN ACQUAINTANCE of mine at DIA, Chris Simmons, developed a tidbit of information about an ongoing effort by the FBI to identify a particular agent spying for Cuba. Like Reg Brown, Chris was a DIA counterintelligence analyst. He shared the tidbit with me and my partner, Karl James. Or as we all know him, Gator.

Gator is a retired special agent of the U.S. Air Force's Office of Special Investigations, an investigative arm of the Air Force that works both criminal and counterintelligence issues. He is a native of Louisiana, where his father worked as a game warden, and Gator grew up on the edge of a bayou. Gator claims that he never had a dog or any other pet while growing up, but he'd leave dinner leftovers near a hollow log by the water outside his house to feed the alligators every day. His nickname around the office has been Gator ever since he first told that story, and I wouldn't feel comfortable calling him by any other name.

Gator and I were a team: a Yankee from Wisconsin and a Rebel from Louisiana. As the DIA's only counterintelligence investigators at that time, the two of us constituted a counterintelligence cell within DIA's Security Investigations and Polygraph Branch. When we considered the tidbit of information that Chris Simmons had shared, we agreed from the outset that the odds were stacked against us, but it wasn't hopeless. I cannot reveal the particular information with which we had to work, but I can say that it was pretty generic stuff. Nothing special.

Fortunately, Gator and I were engaged in nothing more interesting than routine paperwork at the time Chris called. With nothing much better to do at that particular moment, we just naturally jumped at the chance to have some fun by trying to "identify a spy." For now, remember, it was all informal, back-channel communication—certainly not an official investigation.

We brainstormed a bit first. In our business, it's better to frame the problem and develop a logical approach to solving it than to simply jump in and thrash about. Counterintelligence investigators tend to be very thorough and method-ical in the way that they go about their business. It seemed likely, then, that investigators who were working the case had already tracked down virtually every investigative lead that Gator and I might develop in our brainstorming session—and they certainly had a head start on us. But Gator and I decided to give the investigation a shot anyway. We loved the challenge, and the opportu-nity to succeed where others had failed was simply too much to resist.

So we set everything else aside to focus for a short while on someone else's Unknown Subject (UNSUB) case. For us, it was a diversion from the mundane work that presently occupied our time. It was a challenge, a lark. We were just looking to have some fun, and we had little realistic hope of success.

Fifteen minutes later, I identified Ana Montes as the UNSUB. That's all the time it took.

In the counterintelligence business, we know an awful lot about the private lives of our employees. Such is the nature of employment within the intelli-gence community: Employees surrender or waive many of their rights to privacy to qualify for security clearances. Gator and I are therefore privy to a wealth of information about DIA employees as part of our professional work. We know everything about their backgrounds, their families, their friends, their education, and their earlier employment. We know their habits, their hobbies, their addictions, and their fears. We know their doctors, their lawyers, and their various maladies and afflictions. We are intimately familiar with their finances, their clubs, their memberships in organizations, and virtually everything that anyone would ever care to know about anyone else. All of that information, and much more, is available to us at the click of a mouse.

Gator and I also have access to a broad range of DoD information. That data happens to be information to which other agencies, particularly non-DoD agencies, do not have access. We routinely tap into that data from our desktops during the course of the workday to mine it for information that might help us in our jobs.

In this case, we understood instinctively what we had to do, and we simply went to it. With the understanding that our sister agency had probably already run queries on databases and records that we shared or otherwise had in common, we decided to focus our efforts on those databases to which we had unique access. Gator worked on his desktop system and I worked on mine. We queried various databases for matches to the otherwise insignificant tidbit of information that we'd received about the mysterious spy operating somewhere in the intelligence community.

The system produced more than a hundred files for my review. I clicked through them quickly, looking for anything that might intuitively jump out at me and grab my attention. The odds were against that happening, of course, but I was in a race with Gator and I wanted to grab that golden ring before he had a chance to do so.

The routine that I normally follow in conducting such reviews is to perform a quick, cursory scan of the files once and then return to the beginning of my search to review each file slowly, in detail, for content. I was looking first for names I might recognize and then for any comments that might be documented in association with the names. The reference to Ana Montes was perhaps the twentieth such file in the queue.

When her name popped onto the screen, I froze, stunned. Until that moment, honestly, the thought of Ana had not even entered my mind. I was simply too engaged in figuring out how best to query the system to have reflected on my own past experience with Cuban issues. It had been four years, after all, since I had talked to Ana, and a lot had happened since then. I had worked many investigations during the intervening four years and I had traveled to perhaps a dozen or more countries. For all intents and purposes, I'd forgotten about her. The appearance of her name on the screen was totally unexpected. But when I saw it, I realized immediately that I'd found the UNSUB. My jaw just hit the floor. I believe my exact words, at that moment, were, "Oh, shit."

I said it twice. This wasn't fun anymore. The thousand-to-one shot had suddenly come home. This was serious, and a sense of dread washed through me as I stared at the screen. The sound of my voice drew Gator's attention, and he wondered what had happened. Then it occurred to me that I was the only person on Earth who knew that Ana Belen Montes was almost certainly a spy— a major spy—and that, should I suddenly die from heart failure or something, no one on Earth might ever find that out. After all, there were more than a hundred names in the list I'd pulled up. I turned to Gator and drilled him with a rapid-fire recitation of my earlier experience with Ana. He could hardly believe it.

My quick briefing of Gator lasted several minutes. After that, I shifted into another gear. It was time to get down to business. My first thought was to alert the FBI. But I set that action aside to accomplish something that seemed, to my mind, of greater urgency: I had to stop Chris from spreading the word about this case. By sharing the information with me, he had almost certainly led to a major breakthrough, but now that we had a suspect in mind, I didn't want her to hear a word of it.

Chris didn't know that I had identified Ana as a possible suspect, of course, and I refrained from informing him of that fact during our conversation. My rationale was simple. I assumed that Chris was acquainted with Ana professionally, and I didn't know how he might react to the news that she was a suspect. Moreover, I couldn't control his reaction. Chris' office was in the DIAC at Bolling Air Force Base in Maryland, and I was in the Clarendon section of Arlington, Virginia—more than ten miles away. Instead, I simply informed him that I'd identified a possible suspect and that it was imperative to put a lid on the case before the suspect heard that our DIA security office was even looking for an UNSUB. Chris' response was not encouraging. The word on the investigation was already out.

I was amazed by the speed with which word had spread about the case. From Chris, the information had gone to one of his co-workers, and from there to that person's supervisor. From the supervisor, word spread to other colleagues within DIA, all of whom, fortunately, were security or counterintelligence specialists. Within half an hour of Chris' return to his office after he learned the information, employees in all three major office buildings occupied by DIA in the Washington area had learned that an investigation was underway to find a spy in Washington matching Chris' tidbit of information.

This was a problem. Ana was very well connected within DIA. She had been around the agency for about fifteen years, and she knew a lot of people in each of our buildings. She had established excellent networks within the agency, and it would be natural—even expected—for someone to share the gossip about a local espionage investigation that involved Cuba with our senior Cuba analyst. If that were to happen, our prospects of catching Ana in the act of committing espionage would be reduced to nothing. We would be lucky to catch her before she reached the airport en route to Havana.

Even though he didn't know the identity of our suspect, Chris understood the problem. From our conversation, I drew up a short list of the DIA offices whose employees were now aware of the basic fact that the security office was searching for an UNSUB and then ran down the stairs to the fourth floor to see Drew Winneberger, the chief of security at DIA.

Drew is the man who had hired me to work at DIA twelve years earlier, and over the years I had established some credibility with the man. He listened as I quickly briefed him on the problem at hand. Without hesitation, he issued a cease-and-desist order via e-mail to the offices in question and thereby put a stop to the leak. Both of us then followed up the order with secure telephone calls to the supervisors of those offices. Those actions were not a certain remedy, given the limits of human nature, but they were as much as we could accomplish on short notice. We were assured, at least, that no one had attached the name of Ana Montes to the news of the UNSUB investigation. For now, that information was closely retained within the confines of my office. We could only hope that the novelty of knowing something about an ongoing espionage investigation would die a natural death among those who had heard of it before it reached Ana's ears.

6

THANKS, BUT NO THANKS

IT WAS TIME TO NOTIFY THE FBI about the UNSUB. Immediately after returning from Drew Winneberger's office to my own cubicle, I placed a call to FBI headquarters. The supervisory special agent who answered my call seemed genuinely interested in my claim to have identified a possible espionage suspect, but equally concerned that so many people had become aware of the ongoing investigation.

Compromising the integrity of a national security investigation is a serious matter. In addition, although Ana Montes was not officially under investigation by anyone yet, the potential compromise of a case before it even got off the ground required immediate attention. I related every detail that I could recall about the leak and Drew Winneberger's immediate action to put a halt to the information flow. Only after giving assurances that we had the matter under control was I able to focus on the fact that I had identified a possible suspect in the UNSUB investigation. The FBI agreed to meet with Gator and me downtown the next day.

I've worked directly with FBI agents on a variety of issues over a career that now spans many years. I know quite a few of them, and they know me. But most of the agents with whom I work are field agents, agents assigned to the FBI's Washington, D.C., field office who work cases on the streets, as I do. My experience in working with the FBI extended to very few agents at FBI headquarters. So not surprisingly, most of the agents with whom Gator and I met the next day were strangers to us, and we to them.

Had we met on neutral ground to discuss an issue of little or no consequence, our being strangers might not have mattered. But that was not the case. Gator and I were meeting with some of the FBI's leading experts on Cuba to discuss the rather incredible notion that two total strangers from a rather obscure intelligence agency, who possessed no particular expertise in Cuban matters themselves, might have identified almost by accident a major spy operating within the very heart of the U.S. intelligence community. When it came to Cuba, Gator and I were amateurs. FBI agents were the pros.

We had a steep credibility hill to climb in the FBI's office that day. To make matters worse, we carried with us the stigma of having been recipients of a leak of national security information about an espionage investigation in which the FBI naturally had some interest. That was a bad thing. I realized shortly after our arrival that we had some explaining to do.

My first priority was to address the leak and to assure them that it was under control. I gave those present a verbal briefing on the initial leak to Chris Simmons, without identifying his source, and then provided a list of DIA employees who had subsequently learned about the investigation. I assured them that a cease-and-desist order had been issued, and I expressed my hope and belief that DIA employees on the list would move beyond the topic of the investigation during the next few days as they pursued their own work. (That is, in fact, what happened. The leak turned out to be a brief blip on their radar screens that faded with the passage of time.)

Despite the awkwardness of that topic, I was relieved to see we were still operating on a friendly basis. Now I really wanted to get beyond the question of the leak to discuss our discovery of Ana Montes.

I had brought to the meeting a folder filled with information about Ana— her employment history, application forms, background investigation reports, and a report that documented my November 1996 interview with her (which, of course, I had also coordinated with the FBI at that time). I was eager to share what we knew.

I launched into my briefing with great enthusiasm. I must have prattled on for about ten minutes when Steve McCoy, a senior and very experienced agent assigned to the Washington field office of the FBI, politely interrupted my discourse. Steve wasn't one of the agents I knew from the field office, since he wasn't on the squad I worked with most frequently. Until that point in the meeting, he hadn't said a word; he'd listened. But he made up for his earlier silence during the next couple of minutes with several good points that seemed to rebut my case. In the end, even I had to admit that Ana seemed an unlikely candidate for espionage.

Elements of my own briefing came back to haunt me. For example, the fact that Ana appeared to be a model employee only served to weaken the basis for suspicion against her. She was a stellar performer at work who earned numerous awards and early promotion. She exhibited none of the standard espionage indicators—none of the behaviors normally associated with espionage. She had committed no known security violations and had apparently complied with DIA security regulations that required her to report foreign contacts and foreign travel. The bottom line was this: She was not a problem employee.

Also, of course, she was a woman. As I mentioned earlier, 93 percent of Americans prosecuted for espionage in the United States in the modern era (since 1950) have been men. To put it the other way, only 7 percent have been women. In addition, those American women who do engage in espionage typically have done so with male partners. They don't act alone. Among those convicted for espionage, the only exception to that rule in the modern era was a U.S. Army civilian employee in West Germany named Svetlana Tumanova. Her involuntary cooperation with the KGB during the late 1970s and the 1980s was enforced by threats against the welfare of her family in the Soviet Union. Our suspicion, then, that Ana Montes had willingly engaged in a lonely war of espionage against the United States ran completely counter to the weight of U.S. counterintelligence history.

There was even the issue of ethnic background. Historically, Latinos had comprised only 5 percent of Americans prosecuted for espionage during the modern era. Of the women prosecuted for espionage or related offenses, only three were Latinas: Aldrich Ames' wife, Maria del Rosario Ames, and two members of the Cuban Wasp network, Linda Hernandez and Amarylis Santos, both of whom belonged to the network with their husbands. Ana was of Puerto Rican ancestry. Statistically, we could almost rule her out as a suspect based on ethnic background alone.

Additional demographic attributes argued against our suspicions of Ana as well. There was the issue of education, for example. Of all the people prosecuted for espionage in the United States since 1950, less than 14 percent held advanced degrees. Yet Ana had earned a master's degree from the prestigious School of Advanced International Studies at Johns Hopkins University. There was also the matter of her security clearance. Only 15 percent of Americans prosecuted for espionage during the modern era held the highest level of security clearance when they began spying. That level is Top Secret clearance with authorized access to sensitive compartmented information, or TS/SCI for short. That meant she had been screened, vetted, investigated, and judged by competent federal authorities to be a responsible U.S. citizen worthy of the government's trust. Ana not only had held such a security clearance for years, even before coming to DIA, but also routinely accessed a great deal of sensitive compartmented information throughout her normal workday.

In my briefing, I'd also mentioned the best argument of all in Ana's favor. She had successfully completed DIA's counterintelligence scope polygraph examination in March 1994, seemingly with flying colors. It was hard to argue with that. Besides, as Steve went on to tell us, lots of federal workers, contractors, and others in or near the U.S. intelligence community matched favorably against the tidbit of information I had used as the basis for my computer query. Ana Montes' name had appeared on my screen, to be sure, but Ana was certainly not the only match. She appeared to be nothing special.

The meeting was over, and Ana Montes was neither in nor out as a suspect. Steve accepted my folder of materials about her and promised to review it and get back to me. With that, Gator and I were essentially dismissed. Have a nice day.

7

GETTING ON TRACK

I WAS SOMEWHAT DISHEARTENED by the FBI's initial reaction to my suspicions about Ana Montes, though I really should have anticipated their response. They were professionals, after all, who were trained to review information objectively and to reach conclusions after conducting a dispassionate analysis of relevant facts. Intuition plays a role, but a relatively minor role, in such deliberations. In this case, I had posited for their consideration a theory of Ana's involvement in espionage that was based on very few articulable facts. My strongest argument to date, frankly, was a gut-level intuition that I was right. I needed more facts.

Ordinarily, I might have been satisfied to sit back, give Steve McCoy plenty of time to review the information about Ana that I had provided, and await his Eureka! moment. But alarm bells were ringing in my head. If I was correct in my assessment, Ana had already been spying for the Cubans for many years. The damage to national security from an analyst with such top-level access—and a strong professional influence on U.S. policy—had to be enormous. Any delay in neutralizing her activity would result in additional damage, and we couldn't sit by while that occurred. We needed some action.

Unfortunately, facts were hard to come by. Chris Simmons informed me that the person who initially told him about the investigation—a person he and I referred to as Big Mouth to avoid using her name—held additional tidbits of information about the UNSUB spy. She was hesitant to share that information with DIA, however, owing to its sensitivity. She also faced the threat of administrative sanctions if she provided additional information to us.

That information was gold to us. If it matched favorably against what we knew about Ana Montes, it would strongly support our argument that Ana was indeed the spy. I needed that information. To date, I hadn't pushed the issue with Big Mouth. In my overly optimistic frame of mind, I had assumed that the FBI would jump all over my discovery of Ana, immediately open an investigation, and quickly gather the evidence required to support her arrest. I was wrong.

In theory, I could have asked Steve to provide additional information about the UNSUB, but he seemed so upset about the initial leak of information to DIA that, in my view, he wasn't about to volunteer more. I understood his concern. Leaks can compromise investigations, and from his point of view, one leak was more than enough. Big Mouth simply had to come through for us. My immediate priority was to obtain just one more tidbit of information about the unidentified spy from her. We would have to be very persuasive to overcome her natural reluctance to risk the ire of the FBI on our behalf.

I spent the following week clearing my desk of other cases. I also asked Gator to begin the process of gathering additional records concerning Ana's assignments at DIA. I wanted them ready for review by the FBI as soon as they needed them. Gator, of course, had no personal history with Ana. Given our initial reception by the FBI on that issue, he had developed some doubt that she was identifiable with the UNSUB. But my gut-level impressions from the 1996 interview fit together too well with what I had learned already. I just knew that I was right. Frankly, I wasn't going to take no for an answer.

Chris Simmons contacted Big Mouth and persuaded her to reveal a bit more about the UNSUB. She was encouraged by our initial success in identifying someone at DIA as a possible match for the UNSUB, and she offered to provide just one additional bit of information to us—not everything. If that information, too, matched favorably against our unnamed suspect, then she might consider releasing even more information at a later date.

With that additional tidbit in hand, I began to research Ana's life. By the end of the week, I had developed enough additional favorable matches against the UNSUB to convince even Gator that I had the right person. I was traveling a hundred miles an hour in my head, anticipating the tasks that we would have to accomplish during the FBI's investigation. But I hadn't yet received feedback from the FBI's senior agent about my package of Ana Montes material.

Exactly one week after our initial meeting, I called Steve for a progress report. He hadn't completed his review of my materials but he hoped to do so soon. Again, I was disappointed. Still, I hadn't lost heart. I knew that virtually every tidbit of information provided by Big Mouth to date could be matched against information documented in the pile of materials on Steve's desk. All he had to do to find them was to read the material. Eureka! was close at hand.

Another week (six days, actually) went by with no word from Steve. By that time, I was beginning to worry that he'd blown me off entirely, and my frustration was building. I'd found two more points in which Ana appeared to match the UNSUB. My desk was clear of other work. I was ready to rock and roll. Where was Steve?

Unable to wait any longer, I took a trip downtown to his office. I was tired of dealing with him over the phone, and I hoped that a personal visit would nudge him in the right direction. Upon arrival, I called Steve and offered to come up to his office for a short meeting. He concurred, and I hurried to the elevator with high expectations. My heart sank as I approached his desk and observed my folder. The cover had been folded back, but nothing inside seemed to have been disturbed. It appeared that he had opened my file only after I called from downstairs.

I was mistaken. In fact, Steve had reviewed my file in its entirety and had initiated an investigative effort that could prove decisive in resolving the question of whether or not Ana Montes was the UNSUB. As Steve explained, it would just take a little time. I'd have to be patient.

The meeting was very short. I refrained from mentioning the fact that I'd received additional information from Big Mouth and that I'd already matched that information to Ana Montes. I was more convinced than ever that she was identifiable with the UNSUB, and I had additional facts to support that theory. But I didn't want to upset Steve with the fact that Big Mouth had leaked additional information to DIA. I understood intuitively that I could not force my conclusion on him or any other agent. He would have to reach his own conclusion at his own pace. The fact that I was already convinced of Ana's involvement in espionage carried very little weight.

My experience with the FBI a decade earlier, when I spent months trying to convince an agent that Fred Hamilton was a spy, had taught me a very valuable lesson. Hounding an FBI agent (in fact, hounding anyone) in situations like this can be counterproductive. Pressure only causes some individuals to dig their heels in deeper against you. It was better to spoon-feed pieces of information to Steve and to let that little light bulb over his head turn itself on. He'd have to reach his own conclusion.

The following week, I began the process of sharing my case with Steve in small pieces. I did it by fax. Two or three times that week, I faxed little memos to Steve in an effort to nudge him in the right direction. "Take a look at this" and "Take a look at that." But I had to be careful. I didn't want to alienate the guy. And it seemed that he just barely tolerated my interest in the case as it was.

The game I played with Steve at that stage of the investigation of Ana Montes was both uncomfortable and frustrating. But I saw little recourse. The FBI makes its own decisions on whether to open an investigation. They are the big dog on the block, and the rest of the intelligence community depends for its security on the ability of the FBI to make the right decisions. If the FBI declined to open an investigation, DIA did have the option of investigating Ana's activities itself, as my partner and I had done with Fred Hamilton. That's not the preferred option, though. DIA has limited authority and resources to conduct such an investigation. We can't do a proper job of it alone. We need the special authorities, the manpower, the expertise, and the other resources that only the FBI can bring to bear.

In short, the prospects for a satisfactory resolution of the issue against Ana Montes, in the absence of FBI participation, would have dropped to near zero. I couldn't let that happen. I simply had to persuade Steve that Ana was the UNSUB.

I spent two weeks faxing materials to Steve, building my case, and hoping that he would have that Eureka! moment. At the end of that time, I ran out of ammunition. My research produced a match of virtually every data point from the UNSUB to Ana Montes. The facts seemed clear: Ana was the one. She was the UNSUB.

On October 12, 2000, I called Steve again for a status report. He had received my faxes and reviewed my material, but he had not opened an investigation on Ana. Nearly a month had passed since I first brought Ana to the attention of FBI headquarters. I'd been patient as I played my silly little game of spoon-feeding hints to Steve, but now I was out of additional information, out of arguments, and I'd failed to achieve my goal of persuading the FBI to open an investigation. There was only one more thing I could do. I told Steve that I wanted to meet with his squad leader to discuss the issue.

The very last thing anyone wants to do, in a situation like this, is to seek redress from an agent's supervisor. It's like saying, "Hey, I can't deal with you. You must be a dolt, or something. I need to speak with someone who is intelligent, who can understand English, and who can make a rational decision." To go above an FBI agent's head like that is insulting. It is offensive. And it was potentially damaging, professionally, for both Steve and myself. I truly hated doing it, but there appeared to be no logical recourse. Ana Montes was a spy, in my estimation, and I simply had to push the issue.

Gator and I prepared for the meeting with the squad leader. We anticipated the arguments that Steve might present against our theory that Ana was identifiable with the UNSUB, and we discussed the strengths and weaknesses of those arguments. Then I typed up a summary of my findings to date. I produced matching lists, with the UNSUB data points listed on the left-hand side of the paper and the matching data about Ana on the right-hand side of the paper. Tidbit for tidbit, the match seemed obvious. This was going to be a make-or-break meeting. I simply had to convince Steve's supervisor that I was right.

The moment we were introduced, I sensed victory in the air. I could taste it. Steve's supervisor, Diane, was possibly the nicest, most gracious FBI agent I'd ever met. She was personable, perfectly reasonable, and very open. Diane was a person with whom I could do business. I felt confident.

The meeting proceeded pretty much as Gator and I had anticipated, but in a far less confrontational manner than we had feared. It involved a rational and dispassionate exchange of information and views, and it seemed that Gator and I had anticipated virtually everything that Steve tossed onto the table for discussion—except for one item. Unfortunately for Gator and me, that one piece of information appeared to knock Ana Montes right out of consideration as a match against the UNSUB.

The new information took Gator and me by surprise, and we were not prepared to address it at that time. We needed to digest it and cogitate over it. But our case against Ana was clearly in trouble at that point. I could have engaged Steve in a long, drawn-out conversation about the new information, but I decided to keep my mouth shut, simply asking a couple of questions for clarification. The purpose of the meeting, after all, was not to brainstorm with peers in front of Diane, but to persuade her that my findings warranted an investigation.

After the meeting, I was actually much more intrigued than concerned about Steve's new information. I remained firm in my belief that Ana was the UNSUB, and his information didn't shake that belief one whit. But Steve had tossed a new variable into the equation that required an explanation. It was as though he had asked, "If Ana's the UNSUB, then how do you explain this?" I just had to think about it for a while.

At the time of the meeting, however, I was concerned about the effect that Steve's new information had on Diane. If she found it persuasive, then I had a problem. It was my turn. I explained to her that I had matched a wealth of information known or suspected about the UNSUB against the corresponding information that was known about Ana. They were a good match. In a form of reverse logic, I argued that, if Ana Belen Montes wasn't the UNSUB, then we must believe that two persons existed in the world who exhibited precisely the same characteristics and same attributes. That likelihood seemed so small that she must be the UNSUB. I then went over each data point in turn, making observations as I went along.

I thought my presentation was persuasive. It seemed logical, even compelling. But in the end, I lost. More facts were required before the FBI could justify an investigation of Ana Montes. That was that. Our meeting with Steve and Diane occurred on Friday, the thirteenth of October—not my lucky day.

As we prepared to leave the office, Steve asked for a copy of the material I'd brought along to the meeting—my lists matching the UNSUB data points against information that we knew about Ana. His request was both interesting and encouraging. It occurred to me that perhaps my presentation had made an impression upon him after all.

Gator and I huddled after we returned to the office. Steve's new information bothered us greatly. Ana was the UNSUB, of that we were certain. But we had to find an explanation for the information. Something was wrong.

You may wonder why we would second-guess the FBI's better judgment on this matter. The FBI is, after all, the FBI. They are the experts. They know best. If in their judgment a DIA employee is not a good espionage suspect, then logically, we should have received their judgment as good news and rejoiced over it rather than continuing to argue the issue with them. A reasonable response might have been to drop the matter entirely, with a sense of relief, and move on to other work.

The answer comes down to gut instinct—intuition. Gator and I had the advantage of twenty-plus years each of successful experience in the counterintelligence field, combined with an intimate knowledge of DIA and an insider's understanding of the culture, environment, and internal workings of the U.S. intelligence community. I also had the memory of my 1996 interview with Ana

Montes, during which, I was convinced, she had lied to me. Together, we simply knew that Ana fit the attributes of the UNSUB Cuban agent.

The woman was going to be investigated, either by us—DIA security—or by a joint unit of FBI and DIA investigators. Gator and I continued to press the issue because we believed so strongly that we were correct. If our efforts to persuade the FBI of the validity of our viewpoint had failed to date, it must be a reflection of our own failure, not theirs. We had to keep working at it.

I think it was Gator who discovered our mistake. And I emphasize that it was *our* mistake, not that of the FBI.

Steve's new information was based on an analysis of raw data that I had faxed to him a couple of weeks earlier. In reviewing that data after our meeting with Steve and Diane, Gator realized that we had failed to verify it. We had simply dumped the data from one of our systems onto a spreadsheet, assumed that it was accurate, and faxed it to Steve.

Well, there is an old saying you may be familiar with. Never assume anything, because it will make an "ass" out of "u" and "me." We had acted like rookies. In our rush to shovel information to Steve, we had failed to verify the accuracy of data on the spreadsheet. And sure enough, some of the data was inaccurate. We confirmed it three ways from Sunday, and then I called Steve to tell him the news. He wasn't in, so I faxed copies of our data to his office, along with an explanatory note, and hoped for the best.

I came into work the next day, Saturday, October 14, to prepare a memo for Steve that essentially summarized the basis for our suspicion that Ana was identifiable with the UNSUB. The memo ran to eight pages, and I worried about it all day. I barely slept that night. On Sunday morning I awoke early to pace the living room.

Jennifer, my wife, had mounted a couple of my awards on a wall behind the piano, including my National Intelligence Medal of Achievement for work in support of FBI national security investigations. I am not an I-love-me-wall kind of person. I tend to tuck award citations into the bottom drawer of my dresser, but Jennifer had insisted that particular award be placed on display.

As I walked past my award citation on Sunday morning, I couldn't help myself. I'd been through so much during the past month, so much frustration, knowing in my heart, in my gut, and from all of my experience that Ana Montes was a Cuban spy, while others in the counterintelligence community had tried but failed to identify her as the UNSUB. Given the depth of Ana's access to classified material and her influential position within the U.S. intelligence community, the stakes were very high in bringing her to justice. Yet I couldn't seem to persuade a single, well-intentioned FBI agent and his supervisor that I was right.

I broke down, bawling. You can only imagine what went through my wife's mind as I sat at the kitchen table with a cup of coffee in my hand a short while later, sobbing uncontrollably as I vented my spleen at that damned FBI agent. Needless to say, I missed church that day. I was too upset to function. I don't recall saying any prayers, either. But God must have been listening anyway.

The first thing on Monday morning, Steve called me at work. Wow. That was something new: Steve calling me. I'd spent a month trying to get this guy's attention, and he turned it around to initiate a call to me.

He wasn't excited. That's not his style. Steve simply said something about having gotten off on the wrong foot. He then gave me his home phone number and his pager number, adding that since we might be working together for a while, we ought to exchange that kind of information. He'd read my material and found it interesting. But he wanted to check a couple of other things out, and he asked whether I might be free for another meeting.

We were finally on the right track. Steve's turnaround was phenomenal. He had experienced that Eureka! moment over the weekend. It had simply taken a while for him to break out of one paradigm and form a new one. Of course, he wasn't completely sold on the idea that Ana Montes was the UNSUB. He was too much the professional to lurch from one extreme to the other overnight. But he was definitely leaning in that direction, and it wouldn't take much to convince him entirely. I was no longer worried.

From that moment, Steve remained at the nerve center of the Montes investigation. As the senior case agent, he orchestrated the investigative efforts of a large and varied team. It was a tough assignment, and he performed magnificently. His co-case agent, with whom he shared much of the responsibility, was a thirty-year-old agent named Pete with only three years of experience with the FBI. In terms of his FBI career, Pete was, in a sense, still a rookie. But he was also a former cop from Philadelphia. I found him to be well organized, knowledgeable, dependable, and well grounded in common sense—a real asset to the investigative team. We were clearly in good hands.

My job wasn't over. The FBI team still needed me as an action officer at DIA, where Ana continued to work daily throughout the case. That made sense, since I had originally interviewed her and made that first identification with the UNSUB. For this case, Gator would be my invaluable assistant.

8

NO ORDINARY ANALYST

BY THIS TIME GATOR AND I already had a pretty good sense of Ana Montes' life and activities from her official files. The picture of this formerly "invisible" DIA employee would become even clearer as we learned more details in the weeks and months to come. As Steve McCoy had pointed out from the beginning, her life to date was hardly a likely portrait of a spy—at least, not on the surface. Instead, the record showed a compelling picture of career success, built from hard work and talent.

Ana was born on February 28, 1957, at a U.S. Army base in Nuremberg, Germany, where her father was stationed at the time. Her father was a uniformed U.S. Army officer, a psychiatrist in the army medical corps. Both Dr. Montes and Ana's mother were from Puerto Rico, meaning they were U.S. citizens. Ana was their oldest child. She was later joined by a sister, followed by two brothers.

The family returned to the United States when Ana was about a year old, transferring first to an Army post in Knoxville, Iowa, and then to one in Topeka, Kansas. Although Ana spent her formative years in the Midwest, it wasn't exactly a settled life. Army life never is. The children of career officers find it difficult to develop lasting friendships as they are uprooted every few years. It hurts to leave one's friends, so the family itself provides continuity for the children, forming strong bonds to compensate for the transitory nature of military life. Such was the case, I believe, for Ana and her parents and siblings. She remained closest, even as an adult, to the members of her immediate family.

When Ana was ten, the family moved to a comfortable ranch-style home in Towson, Maryland, a tree-lined suburb north of Baltimore. There she lived until she graduated from high school. It was the longest period of permanent residence she had experienced thus far.

I can't resist noting that the area in and around Baltimore is rich in American history. Francis Scott Key penned the words to *The Star-Spangled Banner* aboard a ship in the city's harbor as he watched British frigates fire rockets at Fort McHenry during the War of 1812. Ana's childhood home is only about twenty miles from the spot. The giant American flag that flew over Fort McHenry during the battle, inspiring Key's patriotic words, was hand-sewn just a stone's throw from the fort. It is now being preserved for display at the Smithsonian in Washington, D.C., about sixty miles from Towson. Annapolis, Maryland, home of the United States Naval Academy and the resting place for Revolutionary War hero John Paul Jones, is forty-five miles to the south. Gettysburg, Pennsylvania, location of the famous Civil War battlefield, is an hour to the west. Philadelphia, site of the Continental Congress and home of the Liberty Bell, is only an hour and a half to the north. In a way, Baltimore is situated in the very heart of this country's history—the city is a part of it and is surrounded by it. To me, it's a crowning irony that Ana Montes spent such an impressionable segment of her young life surrounded by the very essence of the American past, only to betray it all later as an adult.

Ana's parents insisted that the children speak only English at home, but Ana still learned some Spanish. (It was only as an adult that she developed near-native fluency.) She must have had a chance to practice it in the summers, when the family often visited relatives in Puerto Rico. Her father strongly supported the position that Puerto Rico should achieve independence from the United States, and he voiced that opinion freely in letters and articles. It was and is a political position shared by many Puerto Ricans. Although a minority have taken a radical path to achieve their goal, Dr. Montes favored a peaceful resolution to the issue. His loyalty to the United States was never in question. Ana's mother worked in Baltimore for the Commission for Equal Opportunity in Employment and was an active member of the Hispanic Society of Baltimore.

Ana attended Towson's Loch Raven High School, which opened in 1972, making her class one of the first at the school. As the date of her graduation from high school approached in 1975, Ana's parents announced their intention to divorce. It was an amicable separation, but divorce can be difficult for children, even those who are entering adulthood. For Ana, the experience likely forced her to mature more quickly than she might have otherwise.

After high school, Ana attended the University of Virginia in Charlottesville, Virginia. She majored in foreign affairs with a concentration on Latin America. Professors described her as a serious student, and her grades reflected that fact. She graduated after four years in the top third of her class with an overall grade point average of 3.28. Her academic advisor, Professor Robert Evans, later described her as "shy but pleasant." To her credit, Ana supported herself financially at college by working as a waitress for the university's Food Services Catering Office, which catered social events sponsored by the university for visiting dignitaries, professors, and administrators.

Following her freshman year, Ana spent the bicentennial summer of 1976 employed by the Public Defender's Office in Baltimore as an investigative assistant. She interviewed low-income defendants to determine whether they were eligible for free legal counsel, questioned defendants about their arrests, and forwarded their accounts to the public defender for consideration. I'm sure she never would have imagined she would be a defendant herself someday.

Ana spent her junior year studying abroad at the Institute of European Studies in Madrid. Sounds nice, but the time spent in Madrid was no vacation. Ana supported herself while in Madrid as a bilingual secretary for Richard Gunther, a political science professor at Ohio State University. She typed up his tape-recorded interviews with Spain's national and regional political leaders. She also tutored a Spanish businessman in English. All of this on top of attending classes and earning high academic marks.

During her senior year, Ana elected to pursue an independent course of study in Puerto Rican politics. That tells us something about her interests at that time of her life, but there is no indication that she had yet turned her attention to Cuba. She sent a synopsis of current political conditions in Puerto Rico to U.S. Senator John Warner of Virginia after graduation. Her paper outlined the possible consequences that current trends in Puerto Rican politics might have on Puerto Rico, the United States, and the international community.

Ana completed her undergraduate work in May 1979. During a four-year course of study, she earned an impressive mix of As and Bs, a record marred by only two Cs. As I went through her records, I noted that one of those Cs was for a class on international law. Granted, it wasn't a criminal law class, but I remember joking to myself that perhaps she should have paid closer attention to that course, given her later troubles with the law.

Ana's next stop in life, not surprisingly perhaps, was Puerto Rico. She lived with an aunt in San Ignacio during the summer of 1979 and found temporary employment for two months in San Juan as a receptionist for a law firm. She performed so efficiently in the latter capacity that the firm decided to expand her portfolio to include administrative duties. When that work slowed, she moved on to a temporary administrative position in the special services division of Sacred Heart University in Santurce. Her supervisor at Sacred Heart, Ada Oliveras de Lugo, was so impressed by Ana's productivity that she considered nominating her for the position of subdirector of the division after only two months.

Instead, another opportunity knocked for Ana Montes, in the form of Quinlan J. Shea, senior management counsel for the DOJ's Justice Management Division. After Shea spotted Ana at work in Puerto Rico, she encouraged her to apply for an administrative position with the DOJ in Washington. Ana got the job. Years later, Shea would describe her enthusiastically as an "outstanding worker and delightful person." She recommended Ana to DIA with glowing comments like, "recruiting her was one of the smartest things I ever did. If you can get her, take her!" Unfortunately, we did.

Before coming to DIA, however, Ana worked at the DOJ's Office of Privacy and Information Appeals for almost six years. She was a real worker, just as Shea attested. Hired as a clerk-typist, Ana performed so well that her supervisor directed her into a special paralegal training program. Thus Ana continued a pattern of success on the job through an arduous work ethic. She became one of three paralegal experts for the DOJ who specialized in the provisions of the 1974 Freedom of Information and Privacy Act (FOIA).

FOIA enables members of the public to obtain copies of U.S. government records. It's particularly handy for those who want to know what the government has in its files about themselves. So would you like to know what the FBI has to say about you? It's simple. Just submit a FOIA request to the FBI, and the FBI will provide you with copies of FBI reports about you. Of course, the government may not provide absolutely everything it has on you. Certain types or categories of information are exempt from provisions of the act, including classified information, confidential information about other people, and so on.

Somebody working for the government has to review every line of the file in advance to determine whether any of the information should be withheld from you. That was Ana's job.

Once again, Ana excelled at her work. Her high rate of productivity made her an ideal employee in the eyes of her supervisors, who routed the most difficult and sensitive cases to her. In March 1980, after completion of a background investigation by the FBI, the DOJ granted her a Top Secret security clearance with authority to access sensitive compartmented information. With that level of security clearance, Ana could review the most sensitive files in the FOIA office—those related to the national security of the United States.

As I mentioned earlier, the government of the United States does not easily grant access to sensitive compartmented information. That information derives from particularly sensitive sources and methods, and it must be tightly controlled to avoid compromising the sources. Only specially cleared individuals are allowed to handle such information, and even they are cleared only for the particular "compartment" or broad category of information needed in their work. Special background investigations are conducted to determine whether persons nominated for this access have established through their past actions that they are responsible, trustworthy, and loyal.

Background investigations are time-consuming and expensive, requiring months of gumshoe effort to gather together the facts and records of a person's life. Federal agencies that request such investigations have limited resources. But Ana appeared to be a good bet. Those who knew her best recommended her without reservation for a position of trust with the United States government.

Ana's performance was consistently rated at the outstanding level. Supervisors praised her "excellent organization and attention to detail" and characterized her as an "exceedingly rare" employee. Even before she completed three years at Justice, she was promoted from the GS-4 pay grade as a clerk-typist to the GS-9 pay grade as a paralegal. She was clearly a stellar performer, a self-starter. In September 1982, the same month she received her promotion to GS-9, Ana began to attend graduate-level classes on a full-time basis at the Washington-based School of Advanced International Studies of Johns Hopkins University. Not many federal employees are capable of holding down a full-time job while completing demanding graduate-level classes at one of the country's premier universities. Yet Ana maintained such a constant, efficient effort at work that office productivity during her two-year course at Johns Hopkins hardly suffered.

In addition to pursuing a master's degree at the School of Advanced International Studies, Ana also volunteered as the unpaid business manager of *INFOBRAZIL*, a newsletter produced by the school's Center of Brazilian Studies. The newsletter job was a challenging volunteer role that included everything from significant editorial tasks to dealing with finances. Ana performed all of that work, held down a full-time job at the DOJ, attended classes, and completed her regular class work for a master's degree. She was a model of self-discipline, drive, and focus.

Ana completed her coursework in May 1984 and continued her employment with the DOJ. She was promoted once again, to the GS-11 pay grade, but a paralegal could not expect much higher pay, even with a master's degree. Future promotion prospects at Justice seemed limited. It was time to move on. Besides, by that time, Ana had accepted yet another responsibility in her life. As we would later learn, while attending graduate classes at Johns Hopkins University and simultaneously working full time at the DOJ, she had been recruited to work as an agent for the Cuban Intelligence Service.

Ana began to look around for other employment opportunities that would provide greater access to classified information that would be of interest to Cuba, while continuing the forward progress of her career. As she searched for a new job, her high-level security clearance gave her a leg up on her competition. In Washington, security clearances can be used like currency. Applicants with an existing government security clearance can go to work immediately in sensitive positions, while those without must go through a lengthy and expensive process. Federal agencies within and around the Washington Beltway like to hire people who already possess the requisite clearances for their jobs.

Ana applied to the Special Research Division of the Library of Congress, the Office of Naval Intelligence, the Arms Control and Disarmament Agency, and DIA. Interestingly, she did not apply to either the CIA or National Security Agency (NSA), two intelligence agencies that administered preemployment polygraph examinations to applicants. DIA did not do so at that time.

Ana's supervisors at the DOJ offered glowing recommendations, including those I quoted earlier. One called her an absolutely outstanding employee. Another said she was one of the best employees their office ever had. She was described as diligent, conscientious, highly productive, creative, and professional in her behavior and attitude. The man who had originally hired her noted that his recommendation of her was total and made with no qualifications, hesitation, or reservation; Ana's character, reputation, and loyalty were above reproach. He highly recommended her for a position of responsibility. One supervisor also noted that Ana was competent in the handling of national security information.

Once at DIA, Ana's upward career trajectory quickly resumed. She was initially hired as an intelligence research specialist in September 1985. An intelligence research specialist is not an analyst; the specialist gathers and packages raw information for later review by analysts, performing a function rather like that of a research librarian. In short order, however, Ana graduated into a full-time analytical position, where she continued to attract favorable notice.

Ana looked like a good fit for the analyst's role. About half of DIA's employee population consists of uniformed military intelligence specialists, who rotate to Washington to add their real-world warfighter perspectives to our analysis. The other half of DIA analysts are civilians. Some are former members of the uniformed military services. A U.S. Army officer might serve thirty years as an intelligence specialist, for example, stationed at various bases around the world. Upon retirement, he'll take his knowledge, skills, and abilities to DIA, where he'll focus on a specific area of interest.

But many DIA civilian analysts, like Ana, have no prior uniformed service. We draw them from universities and colleges all over the country; schools in the Washington area and surrounding region contribute a good number to our ranks. Ana's degree from the University of Virginia was not unusual. Nearby universities share in the culture that surrounds the U.S. seat of government. Students who want to walk the world stage study here. They vie for jobs at the Department of State, populate the offices of every federal agency, and join the ranks of the U.S. intelligence community. They want to play on that stage. The very prospect of doing so, for them, is exciting and fulfilling. And so it was for Ana Montes on her path to DIA.

In 1991, Montes was selected to participate in a fast-track program for future managers. The next year, she participated in the Exceptional Intelligence Analyst Program offered by the director of central intelligence (DCI), an independent study program that allowed her to spend a year working on an analytical project of her own choosing. Very few analysts in the entire intelligence community were chosen for that program.

In August 1996, DIA's Directorate for Intelligence Production was reorganized. Ana was selected to serve as an acting division chief while the dust settled. (That's the position she held when I interviewed her that November.) Her stint in management apparently convinced her that real job satisfaction, for her, was more likely to be found in an analyst's cubicle than in a manager's office.

She so informed her supervisors and thus limited her future promotion prospects, apparently out of sheer devotion to her work.

That year, Ana was also selected as one of three senior members of the intelligence community for a special community-wide project mandated by George Tenet, the director of central intelligence. Exposure at that level cemented Ana's professional reputation throughout the U.S. intelligence community as a player, a professional whose opinions counted. Ana was, at that point, the queen of Cuba within the U.S. intelligence community, the top analyst on the subject. She had arrived. She was not universally popular, but from all she commanded respect.

Ordinarily, analysts with no additional supervisory or managerial duties rise no farther than the GS-13 pay grade, earning perhaps as much as eighty thousand dollars per year. (Technically, DIA employees fall under the equivalent GG system, so Ana was then a GG-13, not a GS-13. Same pay, different system.) Many analysts remain at that pay grade until retirement. But exceptions can be made. For those very few employees whose performance is demonstrably exceptional, the federal government offers the Exceptional Impact Program, or EIP. Just a handful of EIPs are awarded per year. Ana received an EIP promotion to GS-14 in May 1999, and she continued to excel.

During her sixteen years with DIA, Ana consistently earned outstanding or distinguished marks on her annual evaluations. She received special recognition for contributions to DIA's mission on ten occasions, including a performance award of two thousand dollars in cash in August 2000, just months before the investigation began.

Ana specialized in Latin American affairs, with a special interest in Cuba, throughout her career. She served as DIA's principal analyst for El Salvador and Nicaragua from 1986 to 1991, a span of time that coincidentally encompassed much of the Iran-Contra scandal. Lt. Col. Oliver North, USMC, a military advisor to President Reagan's National Security Council, secretly sold parts for U.S.-made surface-to-air Hawk missiles to Iran. He then used the proceeds to covertly support the Contra rebels in Nicaragua against the Cuban-backed government of Daniel Ortega. Ana, the Cuban agent, and Ollie, the anticommunist rebel of the Reagan era, thus worked in secret on opposite sides of the policy fence on the issue of Nicaragua.

While Ana's primary responsibility in the late 1980s was to analyze the military situation in El Salvador and Nicaragua, she also served as a back-up for DIA's full-time Cuba analyst. In 1992, she assumed the position of DIA's primary political/military analyst on Cuba. She had remained on the Cuba account ever since. The combination of her long service as a Cuba analyst, her undoubted expertise, and her many contacts throughout the intelligence community gave her enormous influence.

Ana was adept at using that influence. She could charm and beguile superiors with the best of them. She also had the ability, and exercised the will, to cut offenders to the quick when they dared to question or cast doubt upon her views or to advocate a view in opposition to her own. Several junior analysts learned the hard way about the dangers inherent in crossing her on any issue on which she considered herself to be an expert—or the expert. Some openly admitted that they feared her. We found that it was not unusual to find Ana seated alone at meetings and conferences, apart even from her immediate co-workers. Frankly, she seemed to prefer things that way.

I found it interesting that Ana avoided contact with her co-workers. She rarely attended social functions—birthday parties, hail-and-farewell parties, and so on—with them. That wasn't for her. She could certainly be pleasant, but idle chatter and personal interactions with others seemed to be something that she tolerated, at best, and avoided if she could. Part of that may be attributable to natural shyness, low self-esteem, or an introverted personality. But part of it, I suspect, was a desire to keep those people at a distance, out of her life, and away from her innermost secrets. She was, after all, betraying those people on a daily basis.

It's not easy to betray a friend; it's much easier to betray a stranger. So I suspect that Ana kept her co-workers at a distance to minimize whatever pain she was bringing upon herself by her daily betrayal of those people through espionage. They weren't important to her. Nothing personal.

The picture we built of her private life away from work wasn't much different. Ana was a very private person. To the best of our knowledge, she had no great friends in Washington, despite having lived there for twenty-one years. Neighbors were superficial acquaintances at best. No one was close to her—again, perhaps by design, given the nature of her work for Cuba. She had a number of boyfriends throughout her life, but it wasn't until a man I'll call Bill came along (for privacy reasons, I won't use his real name) that she seriously considered settling down. We don't know what the attraction was between Ana and Bill. Certainly, they shared a professional interest in Latin America. Bill also served as an intelligence analyst for the Department of Defense, and he too was a Latin America specialist, although unlike Ana, he was based in Miami at the time.

It wasn't just that common interest that brought them together, though. They were opposites, and if there is truth to the maxim that opposites attract, there exists a ready explanation for their relationship. Bill was the gregarious extrovert to Ana's aloof introvert. He was wild, spontaneous, and energetic, where she was reserved, methodical, controlled, and serious. He was relatively young (eight years younger than Ana), where she was mature. Bill was somewhat innocent and trusting by nature; Ana was the opposite.

You might think a counterintelligence guy like me would suspect that Ana had no personal interest in the guy at all, that she targeted him coldly for later exploitation or even planned to recruit him as a witting dupe in her espionage activity. A skeptic certainly might think so. At the time of her arrest, Bill was scheduled to begin a new assignment with direct daily access to the United States' war plans.

I don't believe that was Ana's motivation, though. I think she truly wanted to develop a long-term, personal relationship with someone. I suspect she craved some sense of normalcy for herself, for her future. Perhaps she dreamed of taking her retirement nest egg, chucking the espionage bit, and settling down in sunny Miami near her mom some day. Perhaps Bill embodied her hopes for that better, less lonely future. If so, of course, it never came to pass.

Ana Montes was variously described by people in her life as reserved, shy, quiet, aloof, cool, independent, self-reliant, and standoffish. She was called intelligent, serious, dedicated, focused, hard-working, of high moral character, sharp, and quick. On the flip side were descriptions featuring words like manipulative, venomous, unsociable, and ambitious. Still another crop of adjectives included charming, pleasant, confident, and compassionate—as well as businesslike, professional, no-nonsense, assertive, deliberate, calm, mature, unflappable, capable, and competent.

In other words, Ana wasn't much different from many of the people that you know in your own life. At forty-three, her personality was, like most people's, many-faceted and complex. But never, to my knowledge, did anyone describe her as happy, joyful, or fun. There is a saying in the counterintelligence business: There is no such thing as a happy spy. I believe that maxim applied to Ana Montes.

One thing is certainly true: Ana had an awful lot going for herself. She came from a solid, well-grounded family whose love had supported her since childhood. She was smart and had been educated at some of the best schools the country had to offer. She was possessed of an admirable work ethic—one that struck others with awe and that clearly could have carried her to success in any working environment. She was healthy, attractive, and personable. And yet . . .

She was flawed. I am not going to play the role of amateur psychiatrist. I do not pretend to know or to truly understand how Ana's mind was wired. But even I can recognize the obvious when it strikes me squarely in the face. The flaw in her psyche is most evident when I reflect on the close relationship she enjoyed with members of her family. She was closest to members of her immediate family, her brothers and sister and her mother. (As we came to realize, her relationship with her divorced father, who died in 1998, was more complex, and often antagonistic.) In a *Miami Herald* story, Ana's mother Emilia said that the Freudian psychoanalyst "was a very strict disciplinarian. . . . [Ana and Alberto] clashed. Her family was everything to her—the emotional anchor of her life. And yet, though she loved her family members and depended upon them for emotional support all of her life, she nevertheless betrayed them in the most profound way.

You see, Ana was not the only member of the family to secure employment with the U. S. government. As later reported by the *Miami Herald*, Ana's sister was employed by the FBI's field office in Miami, the same office that broke Cuba's Wasp spy network in and around Miami in September 1998. Ana, as we now know, was firmly on the Cuban side of the fence by that time. Her younger brother was also employed by the FBI, as was his wife. Remarkably and tragically, members of Ana Montes' immediate family were employed by the very agency that ultimately arrested her.

How did this small nuclear family, the members of which were bathed in essentially the same homogenous milk of life experiences, produce such contrasting siblings—with Ana committing the crime of espionage for so many years while her siblings worked as loyal government employees? It boggles the mind. Although Ana must have been aware of this incredible disconnect, she still spent holidays, including Thanksgiving, Christmas, and New Year's Eve, with her brothers and sister, their families, and her mother right up to the time of her arrest. She kept virtually everyone else at a distance in her life, but not family.

Ana must have known or suspected, or feared at least, that one day she would be caught. Surely it must have occurred to her that everyone in her life would be affected in the worst way by her arrest, and family most of all. Yet she risked them all, gambling their reputations and the peaceful anonymity of their lives in order to satisfy her needs, whatever they were, to spy. As I mentioned earlier, I learned back in my policing days that there are some people that I just cannot understand.

9

KEEPING HER IN THE BUBBLE

MY BREAKTHROUGH DISCUSSION WITH Steve McCoy occurred on Monday, October 16. He opened a preliminary investigation and was already in the planning stages for his formal request to open a full field investigation. There was much to do. At DIA, Gator and I began a scramble to accomplish the myriad tasks that were necessary to support an FBI investigation. We had already cleared away our other cases as much as possible. Now everything else in our office was put on hold.

It almost went without saying that we wanted to keep Ana totally unaware of the investigation. Counterintelligence investigations are by necessity very discreet efforts to collect information about a suspect's activities around the clock. Ideally, the suspect never realizes that he or she is under the microscope until the final act, the arrest. Until that time, the suspect remains in a bubble of ignorance—happy in his or her assumption that everything is normal. If the suspect is still actively engaged in espionage, he or she will continue to spy, never suspecting that the FBI is watching and recording those activities for evidentiary purposes at trial.

On the other hand, a suspect who detects surveillance or other question-able activity will go to ground in a heartbeat. Espionage is a stressful business. A spy must be forever on the alert for the possibility that someone suspects what is happening. Failure to detect or avoid surveillance means going to jail, possibly for life. If it's committed during a time of war, espionage equates to treason, and the spy can face the death penalty.

So the stakes are high on both sides. It's a game in which the FBI excels, but they often need cooperation from someone on the scene. That was my job as we worked to keep Ana Belen Montes inside the bubble.

In Ana's case, the bubble of ignorance extended to her co-workers and supervisors. We didn't want any of them to become aware of the existence of the investigation. Our rationale didn't stem from a concern that those around her could not be trusted with that secret—all of them had Top Secret security clearances with access to sensitive compartmented information and had proven themselves to be mature and responsible—but from the simple fact that they were human.

Many of the men and women with whom Ana worked had known her for more than a decade. While some may not have liked her particularly, they had established over time a pattern of behavior toward her that was comfortable, predictable, and "normal." We couldn't afford to allow anyone who routinely worked near her or who had worked closely with her for a long time to become aware of the investigation. Such knowledge naturally causes a change in one's attitude toward a formerly trusted colleague, now a suspected spy. Ana would surely notice any sudden change in a colleague's attitude or behavior pattern. She was as sharp as a tack and very alert. So we enlarged the bubble. None of her inner circle of contacts would become aware of our suspicions about Ana Montes' espionage activities until we arrested her at the end of the case.

At the same time that we began establishing—and protecting—the bubble, we also had to move quickly to inform others about the pending investigation. I fully briefed Chris Simmons on the status of our case and alerted him to stand by to support me. He and another DIA counterintelligence analyst, John Kavanagh, would become an invaluable resource for me throughout the operation because of their knowledge of the way that Cuban intelligence operated.

On October 17, the day after my meeting with Steve, I delivered an eyes-only desk note to the front office informing the director and deputy director of DIA in writing that a DIA employee was under investigation by the FBI. The desk note was merely a formality. I assumed that Drew Winneberger, as the chief of security at DIA, had provided a courtesy briefing to the director by secure phone that morning. DIA's director at that time was Vice Adm. Thomas R. Wilson, U.S. Navy.

First thing the next morning, Admiral Wilson called Col. Merritt Smith, the U.S. Army officer who served as Drew's deputy. The admiral sought Colonel Smith's counsel on briefing "the principals"—in this case, the secretary of defense and the director of central intelligence—about the turn of events at DIA. I advised Colonel Smith that it was a little early for that kind of exposure.

My next meeting with Steve occurred on Thursday, October 19. It went well. We addressed every issue in detail and confirmed that Ana Montes deserved our fullest attention. The purpose of our meeting was really to dot some i's and cross some t's in support of Steve's paperwork.

We were clicking along smoothly now, and the excitement was beginning to build even within Steve. His demeanor had changed dramatically from our first meeting, and he actually cracked a joke or two. I sensed that he had to work at the process of being warm and visibly friendly, because it wasn't a natural part of his makeup. To this day, I don't know whether the calm exterior on the guy is the product of a disciplined mind or whether he's simply half-asleep half the time. I suspect he consciously keeps himself under control at all times under all conditions. By contrast, I tend to suppress my personality only until I feel comfortable with a person. After that, stand back. I can become pretty animated. We were an odd couple.

I learned during our meeting that Steve was a law-school graduate. That was good. I knew then that he'd be meticulous about the preparation of paperwork, a crucial piece of any investigation. I also suspected that he would be particular about every other detail along the way, which was good, too. We needed someone like that in charge.

There remained an awful lot of work ahead of us, but taking the time to talk and get to know one another was as important as any task that we might perform that day. Whatever rapport we managed to develop during those first few hours together might have to carry us through some hard times ahead. We needed to build a bond of trust as well, but that would come with time and experience in working together.

From the very beginning of the investigation, since I'd first met Steve at his headquarters, I had been trying to provide the FBI with some perspective about the degree of Ana's access to classified information and to key policy makers. I wanted to impress upon Steve and his colleagues that Ana Montes represented a significant penetration of the U.S. intelligence community. I had worked within that community for more than a decade and had developed an appreciation for the sheer volume of highly classified information to which the average analyst had daily access. But I sensed that Steve and the others didn't quite get it yet and that they had a very steep learning curve ahead of them. They needed a wake-up call. Ana was no ordinary spy.

The following day, I stumbled across a Top Secret document that effectively made my point. Steve was not available that day, so I ran over to his office and requested a meeting with his supervisor, Diane. I handed her an excerpt from the document and directed her attention to the classification, explaining that Ana's access apparently exceeded even my own previous estimate. Then I launched into another of my concerns—the possibility that Ana Montes had high-level contacts within the FBI, just as she did in so many agencies. We needed to get the situation under control before the investigation was blown.

Diane was pleasant and courteous, but she seemed to be confused by my very presence. It suddenly dawned on me that Steve had not yet had a chance to inform his own supervisor about our continued work on Ana Montes, and that Ana was now considered a viable suspect. As far as she was concerned, that issue had been addressed and closed exactly one week earlier. She had no idea what I was talking about.

I slowed my pace and briefed her on my most recent meeting with Steve. Diane had likely been busy all week on some other matters and hadn't had much contact with Steve since we'd last talked. No wonder she seemed confused. From her perspective, I had simply returned to her office like an annoying bad penny. She might have suspected that I was selling this particular package of goods a little too hard, but I assured her that it had been Steve's idea to meet again. Clearly, she needed to get back in touch with her agent. We agreed to talk again the following week, after she had talked with Steve.

With so much to accomplish in the earliest stage of the case, we were moving fast. There wasn't always time to keep everyone up to speed on everything we were doing, a fact that occasionally caused some internal communication problems like that one.

Gator and I were busy during the first few weeks of the joint investigation, running back and forth between our Arlington office and the DIAC at Bolling Air Force Base, where Ana Montes worked. We were gathering records and preparing the groundwork for future investigative efforts.

We had a scare early on when word of the investigation leaked to a Navy counterintelligence analyst who specialized in Cuban issues. Fortunately, the leak was reported to me immediately and I was able to jump on it before the Navy analyst left the building. She knew Ana Montes professionally, and luckily (under the circumstances), she didn't care for her at all. I had a long conversation with the Navy analyst and her supervisor, both of whom understood the need for secrecy. Our list of persons who were aware of the investigation was growing, and we were practically paranoid about leaks.

I normally visited the DIAC no more than once or twice per week, but now I was in the building several times per day. I began to worry about overexposure. I hadn't actually seen Ana since my interview with her in November 1996—nearly four years earlier—but I had to assume she would remember me from that meeting. Now I was deathly afraid that she might spot me during my many forays into the building. One such occasion would not pose a problem. Twice, though, within a short span of time, might put her on alert.

So it was a shock to see her on the elevator. About two weeks into the investigation, on November 1, Gator and I were still running around like madmen to gather materials and information that the FBI would need for its investigation. I'd been through this drill before, and I had a pretty good idea of what the FBI would require, once headquarters approved Steve's request for a full field investigation. There was much to do, and I was lining up my ducks in the DIAC.

One of those ducks involved communications. Gator and I had just visited a trusted engineer in the basement of the DIAC to coordinate future efforts. After the meeting, we stepped onto an elevator to travel to our next appointment. It was lunchtime—not that we had time to eat lunch that day—and a number of people with trays of food boarded the elevator after us. One of them was Ana. To this day, I don't know whether or not she saw me. If she did, she gave no sign. Instead, she settled into a corner and ignored the world—an elevator wallflower. I pretended not to notice her and cursed myself for carelessness. I swore to take precautions from that point on, and I did so. I didn't see Ana again until the day of her arrest.

I had lunch with Reg Brown the next day. Reg and I had had some contact since he first reported his suspicions about Ana to me in 1996, but we hadn't spent much significant time together since then. I casually pumped him for some information about the shootdown of the Brothers to the Rescue aircraft, as though it had just occurred to me. I didn't tell Reg about Ana. He had transferred out of the counterintelligence discipline and into another field of analysis for DIA. Technically, Reg didn't have a need to know about her. So I kept the information to myself. That was not an easy thing to do.

Steve was busy, too. From what I could gather during our daily telephone conversations, he spent a considerable amount of time during the first few weeks of the preliminary investigation performing internal records checks, clearing his desk of other matters, and preparing his request for a full field investigation. That request was a detailed affair and it was very important to us. If successful, the request would serve as the justification for the tremendous resources that the FBI would have to allocate to conduct a proper investigation. It is no small step to take the FBI from a preliminary investigation of an individual to a full field. We're talking money here—and the commitment of scarce resources that have to be transferred away from other potential investigations. Steve's headquarters required a detailed account of his investigation to date, an account that must logically conclude that the FBI's elephantine bureaucracy needed to turn and march in this new direction. It was not an easy task.

By November 7, about three weeks into the preliminary investigation, Steve was prepared to submit his request for a full field investigation to his headquarters. I had been having lots of fun, anticipating future requirements, gathering and collating information, and just running around to prepare for the full field investigation, while Steve had been sitting with his nose to the grindstone in front of a computer terminal, drafting his request. The headquarters building of the FBI was just five blocks away from the Washington field office where Steve worked, so Steve hand-carried his report to headquarters. It was a Tuesday, election day, and voters all over the country were flooding into the polling booths to elect George W. Bush the next president of the United States. Steve was performing his duty as well that day.

We learned after the fact that Ana spent the following Thanksgiving holiday with her brother and his family. At the time, we knew only that she had taken leave for the holiday and we enjoyed a short respite from our duties. My fiftieth birthday fit in about then as well.

The end of November 2000 approached, and Steve still hadn't received authority to open a full field investigation on Ana Montes. We were busy enough collecting and collating information to build a good profile of Ana and preparing for future efforts, but we wanted to do more. Only with the authority of a full field investigation could we seriously attack the problem of monitoring Ana's activities. The transition from a preliminary investigation to a full field investigation required both Washington field office and FBI headquarters personnel to navigate a frustrating, bureaucracy-laden process. It took time.

Still, it appeared that the authority to open a full field investigation on Ana was imminent. On November 27, I sent another desk note to Admiral Wilson. With the opening of a full field investigation in the near future, we were about to cross a threshold. The director now notified his own bosses, the secretary of defense and the director of central intelligence. From that point on, scrutiny of our investigation from those levels of the executive branch became necessary—and acute. We had to show some progress.

With the full field investigation imminent, Gator and I set the stage to monitor Ana's every movement throughout her workday at the DIAC. A million details required our attention. But on the day I sent my desk note to Admiral Wilson, alerting him that the investigation would soon cross that threshold, Ana Montes informed my immediate supervisor that she was about to leave the DIAC.

10

PROJECT 1923

AS WE NOW LEARNED, ANA MONTES had applied months earlier for a fellowship with the National Intelligence Council (NIC), a senior advisory body to the director of central intelligence on regional and transnational issues. The NIC had its offices at CIA headquarters in Langley, Virginia.

The fellowship program enabled selected analysts from the U.S. intelligence community to conduct research for a year on topics of special interest and concern to the DCI, who was then George Tenet. The analysts coordinated their research projects with senior members of the council. For all intents and purposes, however, NIC fellows were empowered to run around the U.S. intelligence community, gathering intelligence from the most sensitive intelligence sources, to satisfy their research needs. They had super access within the intelligence community. Montes was the first DIA employee selected for one of these prestigious assignments. Some of DIA's credibility as a member of the intelligence community was therefore vested in her success.

Montes' management chain within DIA's Directorate of Analysis and Production, as it was now known (it was still familiarly known to all as DI, its former acronym), had scrupulously screened and blessed the application. At the NIC, Fulton Armstrong, the national intelligence officer (NIO) for Latin American affairs, was in frequent telephone and e-mail contact with Ana. As NIO, he was the senior subject-matter expert on Latin American affairs for the DCI, and he welcomed Ana's participation in the fellowship program under his personal tutelage. They had discussed the nature of her research project in some detail, and preparations were already underway to launch Ana further and deeper into the U.S. intelligence community.

Montes' DIA managers and the NIC staff fully expected her to report for duty at Langley as a research fellow at the beginning of the new year, just five weeks away. She had wound up her affairs at DIA and essentially transferred her Cuba account into the temporary care of a subordinate. Incoming requests were now routinely routed from her desk onto that of her subordinate, and she was ready to go. She had only to navigate a few administrative matters before her departure. One of them was a polygraph exam.

Ana's last such exam had been administered by DIA in March 1994, six and a half years earlier. It was outdated. She would need another exam before reporting for duty with the NIC.

We were just six weeks into the preliminary investigation. But we were limited in our ability to keep tabs on Montes without the authority to conduct a full field investigation and without the authority granted by a special court under the Foreign Intelligence Surveillance Act (FISA) to employ intrusive methods to monitor her activities at home and at work. In truth, we were both deaf and blind to her activities at that point. That's why we didn't know a thing about the NIC fellowship until Montes sent a routine e-mail to my boss, Jerry Craig, requesting that he complete a notification form for the NIC on the results of her 1994 polygraph examination.

The revelation of Ana's pending NIC assignment threw us for a loop. Such an assignment meant, for one thing, that all of our advance preparations for future monitoring of Ana's activities at the DIAC were for naught—she would be in Langley. It also meant that my role in the investigation would soon end. There was little that I could offer the FBI if Ana was temporarily out of my purview.

Our greatest concern, though, was the increased access to classified information that Ana would enjoy while assigned to the NIC. We could not imagine that George Tenet would even allow her to report for duty at CIA headquarters. Yet nothing would be more likely to alert Ana to our investigation than the last-minute derailment of an important assignment, blessed throughout the community, accepted by her own management chain and that of the NIC, and in the works for months. A last-minute cancellation would surely cause her to go to ground. This was a major problem.

Ana knew that she would have to submit to another polygraph examination before reporting to the NIC. With her e-mail, she was purposely attempting to skirt the system by requesting Jerry Craig to complete the form regarding her earlier polygraph exam and forward it to the NIC. She understood from her years of government service that the filing of such a form was probably an administrative rubber stamp. She hoped to slide it into the paper mill at the NIC instead of actually submitting to a new polygraph examination. But someone up in Langley was on the ball. He or she realized upon receipt of the form that Ana's polygraph was outdated and sent it back to DIA. Through an exchange of e-mails with Jerry Craig, Ana then agreed to submit to a DIA-administered polygraph test to satisfy the NIC's requirement. She was scheduled to return to work from her Christmas vacation on Monday, January 3, 2001, so her polygraph at DIA was scheduled for the next day. She would report to the NIC at Langley the next day, January 5, 2001.

On the surface, it was all very routine. But behind the scenes, we were scrambling.

Almost immediately after Montes' first e-mail to Jerry Craig, Drew Winneberger and I traveled to the Pentagon to brief Admiral Wilson, the director of the DIA, on the Ana Montes investigation. The admiral maintained his primary office in the Pentagon, where he served a variety of masters.

Among other things, the DIA director provides intelligence support to the policy side of the Defense Department house as an advisor to the secretary of defense. He provides direct intelligence support to the warfighter side of the house as the intelligence officer for the chairman of the Joint Chiefs of Staff. He also, of course, responds to the intelligence needs of the major combatant commands (for example, the U.S. Central Command, which directed military operations during Operation Desert Storm and would later do so for Operations Enduring Freedom and Iraqi Freedom) and other major military commands (for example, the Transportation Command, which is responsible for the transportation needs of U.S. forces).

The director wears two hats. In addition to his role as DIA director, he's also the director of military intelligence (DMI), with oversight responsibility for the military intelligence budget shared by the Army, the Navy and Marine Corps, the Air Force, and other defense agencies that perform intelligence functions. He produces studies, estimates, and other intelligence products for decision makers in the government, including but not limited to members of Congress and the president. It's for all of these reasons that the director has his main office at the Pentagon.

This was my first face-to-face meeting with Admiral Wilson. The deputy director of DIA, Mark Ewing, was also present. Drew introduced me, and I then conducted the briefing, detailing for the director and his deputy the facts that supported our suspicion that Ana Montes was identifiable with the FBI's UNSUB. The facts were not conclusive, but they were compelling. Admiral Wilson clearly grasped the gravity of the situation. He planned to notify the secretary of defense and speak with DCI George Tenet. It went without saying that Drew would keep the admiral abreast of events in the case as they unfolded.

Admiral Wilson and George Tenet discussed the Montes situation, and Tenet, in turn, contacted the FBI about the case. On December 4, 2000, Tenet hosted a meeting attended by Wilson and an assistant director of the FBI. I was not present for that meeting and was not privy to their discussion. But I imagine a consensus was reached to the effect of: This is serious and we'd better get on top of it. Let's get this situation under control.

The pressure was on, and yet we still lacked authority to conduct a full field investigation and FISA authority to employ intrusive methods to collect information about Ana Montes' activities. We were limited by law to conducting records checks, performing some physical surveillance, and conducting interviews, but to keep Ana from suspecting our activities, none of the interviews would be conducted until sometime after the arrest. Our hands were effectively tied.

Meanwhile, Ana's assignment to the NIC continued to move forward. No decision to cancel her assignment had been made, and the FBI still had some time to gather information about her activities. Time for action, though, was running very short. Ana was due to report to the NIC in exactly one month.

George Tenet could have nixed Ana's assignment to the NIC at any time, of course, and that would have been that. The problem of Ana's gaining access to even more information than she enjoyed as a DIA analyst would have been fixed. But again, such an action would have alerted her and almost certainly led to a premature and unsatisfactory conclusion. No one wanted that. Everyone wanted to catch her in the act of committing espionage—if, in fact, she was still engaged in that activity.

The latter issue was something that hung like a cloud over everyone involved in the early stages of the Ana Montes investigation. We did not know whether she was still actively engaged in espionage. We felt confident that she was the UNSUB and that she had therefore engaged in espionage for the Cuban

Intelligence Service in the past, but whether she continued to do so in the present was unknown.

In fact, there was good reason to believe that Ana might be either dormant or permanently inactive. In the wake of the FBI's 1998 arrests of members of Cuba's Wasp network, Chris Simmons and other counterintelligence analysts assumed that any other agents still on Cuba's books would have gone to ground—temporarily inactive—until the coast was clear. Ana Montes could have been among them. We knew, too, that Ana had been suffering from anxiety and sleeplessness for several years, since about July 1997, and that she continued to consult with a counselor and receive medication to resolve those medical issues. (Employees with a security clearance are required to tell us about mental-health treatments.) It was entirely possible that my interview of Ana in November 1996 was a source of stress that led, in part, to her anxiety and sleeplessness.

As recently as late 1998 or early 1999, Ana had talked of getting out of government service and seeking a job in the private sector—perhaps in a think tank, a number of which dot the landscape of the Washington metropolitan area. It wouldn't have surprised us a bit to learn that she had quit the spy business altogether and that we had opened a case on a former, rather than an active, agent.

Still, our guts told us that she was still active. She was far too valuable to the Cubans, given her access to classified information and her influential position within the intelligence community, to terminate her espionage altogether. More likely, if the Cubans were concerned about her health or her security as their spy, they had simply told her to go quiet for a while. We believed that she would show her true colors eventually, providing, of course, that circumstances would allow us to investigate her at all. Everything seemed to hinge on the DCI's decision whether to allow her into the NIC.

Personally, I could not imagine George Tenet allowing her to report for duty at Langley. To do so would have been irresponsible, not to mention politically untenable. How could he have later defended such a decision to members of Congress and to the American public? To me, it seemed like a no-brainer: She wasn't going to the NIC. So I started to shop around for something, anything that might be used to at least delay that assignment until the DCI made his decision.

Our problem was compounded by the fact that we could not inform anyone within Ana's chain of command at the DI about our need to delay her assignment to the NIC. Had we been able to talk to her managers, we could have concocted a simple scenario to put the brakes on her departure from DIA. But we couldn't risk informing anyone who worked with her or supervised her that she was under suspicion. All of them remained inside the bubble of ignorance, where they could be of no help to us. We explored the possibility of using the NIO for Latin American affairs, or perhaps someone else at the NIC, to slow the processing of her assignment. That option was similarly ruled out, however. We were on our own.

Whatever scenario was employed to delay Ana's NIC assignment, it would have to come from within DIA, and it could not involve anyone who knew her or who supervised or regulated her work, since they were inside the bubble. The scenario would have to fool not only Ana, who was a very savvy employee of the federal system, but also everyone in her chain of command, including the deputy director for intelligence and everyone in the NIC, including the NIO for Latin American affairs. No one could suspect that anything unusual had happened to Ana, least of all Ana. No one could suspect that anyone, particularly an investigator for DIA security, had manipulated events behind the scenes. As Steve McCoy's action officer at DIA, it was up to me to make this happen. Fortunately, I'd done things like this before.

In this case, luck appeared in the form of my old friend Bobby Speegle. Bobby was a retired Air Force colonel and a longtime civilian employee of DIA who happened to be one of my wife's co-workers in DIA's Office of the Inspector General. He is an experienced intelligence professional whose quiet demeanor and remarkable physical resemblance to the late Winston Churchill endear him instantly to friends and strangers alike. His appearance is that of a kind and gentlemanly old duffer, but I know Bobby to be as wily as a fox. I like him principally because he is a can-do kind of person. He gets the job done. Bobby Speegle was exactly what I needed.

Within the Office of the Inspector General, Bobby was responsible for the conduct of investigations to resolve intelligence oversight issues against DIA employees. On the rare occasion when a DIA employee violated federal restrictions governing the collection of information by intelligence community members, Bobby stepped in to establish the facts of the matter. Ana, it seemed, had violated such a restriction, and he was already in the early stages of his routine investigation. Her infraction was a minor affair, but it seemed ideally suited to my purpose of delaying her assignment to the NIC without alerting her to the fact that "Security" was pulling strings behind the scenes. I didn't want her to so much as suspect that she was being manipulated in any way.

I couldn't think of a better qualified intelligence officer than Bobby to help me pull this off. I made an appointment to see him on December 12. Time was growing short. Ana was scheduled to leave the area for her vacation on the twenty-second. We had ten days to accomplish our mission of delaying her NIC assignment.

Bobby had already sent a memo to the deputy director for analysis and production, the senior civilian within Ana's chain of command, advising that he had initiated Project 1923. This was simply the official name for an inquiry to resolve concerns that Ana had violated regulations governing contacts between members of the intelligence community and members of the media. The memo was dated December 7, 2000, so it was a very recent notification of action.

The investigation concerned an incident that took place some months earlier. In August 2000, Ana had read an article in *Soldier of Fortune* magazine that documented the experiences of former U.S. Special Forces members who occasionally traveled to Cuba on vacation to parachute into the ocean with Cuban Navy Special Forces from hovering helicopters. She had sent an e-mail to *Soldier of Fortune*, identifying herself as a DIA employee and expressing interest in contact with the author of the article. A short time later, the author called her, and they engaged in a conversation from which Ana gleaned the information that interested her. The author seemed agreeable to a formal interview, so Ana made arrangements for someone else to talk to the man.

That action exemplified Ana Montes, the analyst. It demonstrated her initiative to accomplish an analytic mission for DIA. But it also violated a procedural regulation. Contact with members of the news media is heavily regulated within the intelligence community. The standard practice is to avoid members of the media altogether. This is for their own protection, lest people suspect that they work for U.S. intelligence. In fact, no such service is ever performed by the media on behalf of the U.S. intelligence community. If Ana had taken an interest in the topic of an article, she should have found some way to gather more information without contacting the author. Someone complained about her action, and Bobby's Project 1923 was launched.

The fact is, this sort of thing happens from time to time. Clearly, Ana Montes was not attempting to use a member of the media to collect intelligence from anyone. She just wanted to debrief him. But she committed an infraction by directly contacting the guy, and that infraction was properly placed under investigation by Bobby Speegle. The facts developed during Bobby's investigation would be dutifully reported to DIA's Office of General Counsel, and perhaps further up the chain of command to the Office of the Secretary of Defense. But the infraction warranted no more than a slap on the wrist, and everyone in Ana's chain of command knew it. Her violation was not uncommon.

Still, I thought it might be useful. So I briefed Bobby on the case and then spent an hour or so brainstorming with him. We developed a plan to use Bobby's investigation to our advantage. I briefed the plan up and down the chain of command, and it was approved for action, with one addition. We were now required to delay Ana's polygraph examination as well—also in a way that would avoid alerting her. And, of course, a significant delay would be preferable to a short-lived, temporary delay.

Bobby and I consulted again. In the meantime, the investigation continued to cook along. In mid-December, FBI headquarters provided authority to conduct a full field investigation, a decision that released significant resources to support the investigation and allowed Steve to bring additional investigative methods to bear. Many members of Steve's squad thereafter supported the Ana Montes investigation to the exclusion of lower priority cases, and Steve had authority to task FBI technicians and other specialists to support his case. The FBI was rolling.

At DIA, we were active, too. To get ready for the time when FISA authority would be granted to collect information on Ana's activities at work by more intrusive means, we gathered blueprints and maps of Bolling Air Force Base and prepared to electronically monitor Ana's activity while at work. Gator periodically gathered and perused telephone logs, e-mail records, and computer files in an effort to keep a finger on Ana's pulse until we received authority to employ intrusive methods. ("Intrusive methods" include techniques such as electronic surveillance, physical searches of home and work locations, and so on.) This was a very busy time. The pressure to stay on top of the situation was enormous, now that the director of DIA, the secretary of defense, and the DCI were all engaged on the issue.

To top things off, Gator and I also handled other counterintelligence issues for DIA at the same time. We were the only counterintelligence specialists within DIA's Security Investigations Branch, so we filled our rare slack moments during the Montes investigation with unrelated issues that affected the security of DIA. It was a madhouse.

On Monday, December 18, we were ready to launch our mini-operation to temporarily delay Ana's assignment to the NIC and simultaneously postpone her polygraph—all without alerting her. People above my pay grade were begging us to delay Ana's assignment to the NIC by even a day or two, perhaps a week.

I contacted Bobby Speegle; we rehearsed every facet of the plan, and then we launched. Ana planned to depart the Washington area on Friday and join Bill in Cancun, Mexico, for some fun in the sun. She expected to take her polygraph exam the day she returned then head straight for Langley and her NIC assignment. If all went well, we would nix the NIC for the time being and delay her polygraph, while ensuring that everyone remained securely inside the bubble of ignorance.

Bobby, of course, would have known nothing about Ana's NIC assignment and her date with the polygraph examiner had I not informed him. That's just the way the system works. As a member of the inspector general's staff, Bobby worked in a world that was administratively separate from the Directorate of Analysis and Production, within which Ana worked. He couldn't be expected to know everything that went on within DI. It would have seemed odd if he had walked into the directorate fully knowledgeable about its business. The people with whom Bobby was about to deal on my behalf were very experienced in the ways of the agency. It would be hard to pull a fast one on them without raising eyebrows. So we had to make Bobby's knowledge of the facts plausible, and quickly.

Our first stop was Marty Scheina, the chief of the Latin America Division and Ana's second-level supervisor, one step above her branch chief. Marty was also the DIA manager who originally hired Ana in 1985.

Bobby's meeting with Marty was ostensibly a courtesy call on the division chief of the subject of his intelligence oversight investigation, Ana Montes. A visit of this sort was expected before Bobby launched into his investigation of Marty's subordinate. Bobby's true mission, however, was to "discover" from Marty that Ana was scheduled to go to the NIC soon. With that information in hand, Bobby's next task was to suggest a delay in that assignment until sometime after the intelligence oversight investigation, to avoid the appearance that DIA was sending an analyst over to the NIC who carried the baggage of an on-going investigation with her. That would be a bad precedent to set, since Ana was the first DIA analyst to participate in the NIC fellowship program.

It sounded good in theory. In practice, it almost went that well—but not quite. Bobby was successful in eliciting from Marty the fact that Ana was scheduled to go to the NIC, but his suggestion to delay that assignment fell as flat as a pancake. In fact, Marty reacted rather angrily to it. He had been around long enough to know that Ana's infraction was minor. He even admitted to having knowledge of her contact with the author of the *Soldier of Fortune* article. It was no big deal, and he argued against any delay of Ana's assignment on those grounds. Bobby left it at that. At least he had accomplished our first objective.

Bobby reported back to me on his meeting with Marty. We agreed that Bobby should brief his own boss, Bud Uthe, the DIA's inspector general, in order to preempt any effort by Marty or Marty's chain of command to torpedo Bobby's suggestion. That's how the bureaucratic game is played, not only in DIA, but everywhere. To win, you must understand the culture of the agency in which you operate, the personalities that populate that agency, the internal politics and dynamics of that population, and the common tactics that are used to maneuver around the playing field. Because of the need to maintain the bubble around Ana, we found ourselves in the position of manipulating the master manipulators, people who really knew their way around DIA. We had to anticipate their every move.

Bud Uthe agreed to back Bobby's suggestion. It made sense to delay the assignment anyway. It really wasn't such a good idea to send someone over to the NIC who had a cloud over her head. If anyone called to complain about Bobby's position, he would put his full weight as inspector general behind it.

As it happened, Bobby already had an appointment to see Caryne Wagner, deputy director for analysis and production, on an entirely separate issue. Caryne was at the top of Ana's chain of command, several managerial levels above Marty Scheina, a distant subordinate. Bobby decided to weave the Ana Montes situation into the conversation with an offhand remark. "By the way . . ."— that sort of thing. His hidden purpose, of course, was to obtain agreement from the senior manager in Ana's chain of command that the NIC assignment should be delayed.

We believed she would go for it. Our only real concern at that point was that Marty might have beaten us to the punch. A savvy bureaucrat, Marty certainly would have alerted his own managers to Bobby Speegle's proposal to delay Ana's assignment. That report would have begun filtering its way through the chain of command, first via telephone calls, and then, most likely, by e-mail, all the way up to Caryne Wagner. If the information had already reached her, then she would be prepared to counter Bobby's suggestion. Bobby would have to deal with the situation, whatever happened.

No problem. Caryne Wagner had formerly served on the staff of a congressional intelligence subcommittee. She was very attuned to the concept of preparing the political battlefield before launching an initiative. Ana Montes represented DIA's first foray into the NIC fellowship program, and she wanted Ana to be an astounding success. Success would then breed more success. A cloud, on the other hand, would not do. So the request for a small delay of perhaps a couple of weeks, until Bobby could wrap up his inquiry, seemed reasonable. She would pass the word down the chain to Ana's supervisor. So far, so good.

Bobby's next move was to call Ana. Again, there was a pretext for the call. It was ostensibly a courtesy call, just touching base with his suspect to introduce himself before he officially launched his inquiry. That was common practice in the polite world of intelligence. This time, Bobby's true objective was to learn from Ana, supposedly for the first time, that she was scheduled for a polygraph examination. He would then set the stage for a delay in the exam itself.

During our brainstorming sessions, we had realized that Bobby and Ana were taking their vacations on nearly the same dates. Ana was scheduled to return to work on Monday, January 3, 2001, and then undergo her polygraph the next day. Bobby intended to return to work on January 4. We wove those facts into our scenario as well.

Ana, of course, had been fully informed about the intelligence oversight investigation. We assumed that Bobby's December 7 memo had made its way to Ana and that she would already have discussed the entire issue with her branch and division chiefs. Again, that's just the way the system worked. We presumed they would have prepared themselves for Bobby's visit, long before he first contacted Marty.

Bobby's visit to Marty would have been similarly dissected and discussed with Ana. She would be fully prepared for Bobby's call. Everyone understood how the game was being played.

But we had some tricks up our sleeves. In their phone conversation, Bobby told Ana that he was aware of her pending assignment. He congratulated her on her selection and wished her the best of luck. But first, they would have to resolve this little matter of the intelligence oversight violation. Bobby said that the violation itself appeared relatively minor on its face, but that he would have to go through the process of gathering facts to establish the truth. He assumed that she would prefer to resolve the issue as quickly as possible. Ana agreed. To that end, Bobby offered to expedite his own inquiry. He was terribly busy for the rest of the week, and thereafter he would be on vacation, but he suggested they get together for a formal interview as soon as he returned from vacation—on January 4, say, at nine o'clock in the morning in Bobby's office at the DIAC.

Bobby's proposal, of course, was music to Ana's ears. The guy was reasonable, accommodating, and he even minimized the severity of the intelligence oversight violation. This would be a breeze. She immediately accepted his offer. Then there was a pause, as we expected, as she checked her schedule. January 4, of course, was the date of her polygraph examination. She was scheduled to report to the polygraph suite at DIA's Arlington, Virginia, facility at eight o'clock that morning. She had a schedule conflict. Bobby waited to hear all about it.

Ana informed Bobby that she was scheduled to take a polygraph during the morning of January 4, to satisfy a requirement established by the NIC. Was there another date and time that might be convenient for the interview?

That was the pitch. We'd backed her into the corner, and then made an offer she couldn't refuse. Bobby expressed mild surprise and disappointment at not being able to meet with Ana as soon as he got back to work on January 4. It was too bad about that polygraph appointment. He suggested, though, that she might want to check with the polygraph branch about their policies regarding administering exams to employees who were under investigation. It was Bobby's understanding that our polygraph examiners didn't like to administer exams in that situation, because employees tended to become distracted and upset about their investigations, and those emotions could mess up the polygraph charts. Bobby was pretty sure that the polygraph examiners wouldn't even administer an exam, under those circumstances. He suggested that she check with them.

As we expected, Ana jumped at this chance to get out of a polygraph examination. She had passed a polygraph before. For all we knew, she might have been trained by the Cubans to defeat our polygraph examination. Perhaps she had no fear of it. But she was also human. No human being on earth would choose to submit to a polygraph examination if there was an opportunity to get out of it.

We had a back-up plan, in case Ana did not take the bait. But the back-up plan would have been used only as a last resort, because it ran a greater risk of alerting her. Had Ana not taken the bait, then we would have waited a couple more days before sending an e-mail to her, suggesting that DIA security was aware of the existing investigation and wished to delay the polygraph examination. I didn't like that plan, and I'm glad we didn't have to use it. Somewhere in the back of her mind, eventually, Ana would have questioned how the polygraph examiners became aware of the existence of Bobby's investigation. Ordinarily, they wouldn't. That alone might have been enough to cause her to go on alert.

Fortunately, we were right. Ana didn't hesitate to skip the exam. She informed Bobby, on the spot, that she would commit to an interview in his office at nine o'clock in the morning on January 4. She would also discuss the issue of her investigation with the polygraph examiners.

Bobby called me immediately to advise that our plan had worked. I got off the phone to find my boss Jerry Craig. I discovered that Jerry and Drew Winneberger, the chief of DIA security, were in the lobby area outside the entrance to our office suite, near the elevators. A Christmas party was in progress, and they were chowing down on goodies in the lobby while I sweated bullets in my office, trying to manipulate Ana Montes and her supervisors into playing things our way. Jerry was seated on some kind of makeshift chair, and I nearly bowled him over in my haste. I needed his help to follow this through to a successful conclusion.

I simply told Jerry that we expected an e-mail on his system pretty soon, and that he'd better get back into his office to receive it. I gave him one of those you-know-what-I-mean looks, and jerked my head back toward his office.

Ana had timed it perfectly. We no sooner walked through Jerry's office door than a ping sounded on his computer. It was an e-mail from Ana, looking for guidance just as Bobby had suggested.

In his reply, Jerry affirmed his policy regarding the administration of polygraph examinations while an employee is under investigation. It simply was not done. Ink tended to spray all over the place, and the average employee could not satisfactorily complete an exam under those circumstances. Ana's polygraph would, indeed, have to be rescheduled for some time after the investigation was completed. Jerry copied Bobby Speegle on his response to Ana and asked Bobby to apprise him whenever the inquiry was done. That was that.

The beauty of our plan was that security's fingerprints were not on it. No one would have suspected that Scott the counterintelligence guy was pulling strings behind the scenes, because we wove our agenda into an existing condition. That's how this job is done.

Upon reflection, Ana would have to blame herself for her temporary predicament. She was the one who committed the intelligence oversight violation, after all. She had set her own destiny in motion. I had simply nudged it in the right direction. Her chain of command had directed the delay in her NIC assignment—a delay that we now controlled. Its duration could be lengthened or shortened according to our needs; all we had to do was call Bobby. Ana herself had initiated the effort to delay her own polygraph. Bobby had simply planted the seed. She did the rest.

We suspected that Ana would report the entire sequence of events to her Cuban handlers, if she were indeed an active agent. It had to appear—to them as well as to Ana—to be a natural and predictable progression of events. Her handlers might suspect that DIA counterintelligence was operating behind the scenes, manipulating events. However, an examination of the facts, as known and presented by Ana Montes, would force the conclusion that Ana had simply messed up with the magazine article. She had brought the heat down on herself. Besides, she ultimately benefited from a delay in the polygraph examination. She would now have more time to prepare for the examination, whenever it was finally administered, and that was a good thing, not a bad thing. We were confident that Ana and her handlers had not gone on alert.

At the same time, Ana remained well aware of the continuing risks she ran as an agent. That Thursday night, December 21, she went to Mass—a break with her usual routine. She usually attended Mass on Sundays, at St. Thomas Apostle Church in northwest Washington, D.C. (The same church, as it happens, that was used by Aldrich Ames as a signal site to communicate with his Russian intelligence handlers.)

Now, it's not unusual for Catholics to go to Mass before Christmas. Maybe Ana was simply taking advantage of her last night in town to attend Mass alone. But still, it seemed unusual for Ana, who did not ordinarily go to the church at night in the middle of the week. I would have expected her to wait for the holidays, when she could go with her mother and sister on Christmas Eve or Christmas Day.

We began to look into it. And we found a coincidence, which bothered me, because I don't put much stock in coincidence. December 21 is the feast day of Saint Peter Canisius, a sixteenth-century Jesuit priest who is sometimes called the second apostle of Germany for his work in restoring Catholicism to that country. More relevant to this story, Canisius also served briefly as a Vatican spy. Or rather, as a Vatican secret agent of sorts. After the conclusion of the Council of Trent, the pope named him as a secret nuncio, charged with delivering the council's decrees throughout Germany. Despite the danger, Father Canisius succeeded in his mission. He was the perfect agent.

Is it possible that Ana Montes went to church on the feast day of Saint Peter Canisius to seek his protection and his blessing for her work as a spy? "From one secret agent to another, hey, would you please give me a hand? Keep me from getting caught." Is that what she was doing at Mass that night? I don't know. But I am uncomfortable with coincidences.

When Ana returned from her vacation, she met with Bobby Speegle as planned. The interview went well, and Bobby suggested that he might complete his inquiry by the middle of January. Routine processing of his report might require an additional week or two, as it made its way through the approval chain and then over to security for adjudication. After that, his report would be forwarded to the polygraph shop for their review. At that point, the polygraph examiners should be prepared to administer an exam. He would expedite the entire process for her. Ana was a happy camper.

The powers that be in pay grades above my own had asked us to buy a delay of at least a day or two in Ana's move to the NIC—perhaps a week, if it could be managed. A delay meant breathing room, time to think, time to develop additional plans for dealing with Ana Montes, and time to implement those plans as necessary. We had bought them at least a month, and that could be stretched to six weeks without alarming Ana.

Still, it was only a delay. Ana still expected to move on to Langley and her assignment at the NIC. No final decision had been made to derail that assignment, or to allow her to proceed to the NIC assignment, for that matter, while still under investigation. No one knew what the future would bring, but at least we had some time to prepare. If, as I suspected, a decision was made soon to cancel her assignment to the NIC altogether, then we would have to devise another operation behind the scenes to terminate that assignment—again, without alerting her that she was under suspicion.

We were happy. But perhaps it was we, and not Ana, who remained ignorant. Her interview with Bobby Speegle had occurred at nine o'clock on the morning of January 4, 2000. Around 4:30 that afternoon, close to her usual quitting time, she placed a call to an FBI analyst at headquarters whom she had met several years earlier. As it happened, that analyst was currently supporting the Washington field office on an important case: the Ana Montes investigation. The call at 4:30 must have reached a voice messaging system, because it lasted only a minute. But she didn't give up. The next morning, first thing, she placed a call to the same number again. Ana Montes was reaching out to an FBI contact, and we didn't know why.

11

DERAILING A PLUM ASSIGNMENT

AS IT TURNED OUT, ANA MONTES' CALLS to her contact at the FBI in early January would remain one of those loose ends that occur in any case. We immediately informed Steve McCoy and his team that she had made the calls, but our worst fears were not realized. While Ana was clearly being vigilant, she didn't know the investigation was underway.

Meanwhile, we awaited the submission of paperwork to the FISA court to obtain authority for the use of intrusive methods to collect information about Ana's activities, both at work and off the job. Counting the preliminary phase, the investigation had been running for nearly three months, but we were still extremely limited in our efforts to monitor Ana's activity. We couldn't catch a spy unless we could see what she was doing. The only thing we had in our bag of tricks was physical surveillance, and even that seemed spotty at times. Nothing unusual had been noted.

We suspected that Ana's Cuban handlers had cautioned her against removing materials from work, in any event. By now we believed that she had worked for the Cubans for many years. That fact alone suggested not only that she was of great value to them but also that they had reason to trust her deeply.

In the espionage business, value and trust can change the entire dynamic of the relationship between an agent and his or her foreign handlers. Low-level agents of limited seniority are expected to provide hard materials, like paper reports, disks or CDs, video images, photos, or other media. Such items can be evaluated independently from any commentary or supplemental verbal information that the agent has to offer. Low-level agents, even those who provide hard materials of great value, are not trusted to provide accurate information without supporting documentation. By contrast, high-level agents—those with longevity and a proven record who are also considered motivated and reliable—may provide valuable verbal reports, even without supporting documentation. Ana Montes likely fit into that category of agent. She might not need to take anything home from the office to do her spy work. Especially after the arrest of Cuba's Wasp network, that would certainly be the safer course.

Then, too, Ana had been in some danger of exposure at one point in her career. My interview with her in November 1996 must have given her and her handlers cause to pause—or at least the motivation to adopt more secure methods of communication and to avoid risks like removing materials from work. It seemed likely, then, that her handlers might have encouraged Ana to take information out of the workplace in her head then record her thoughts in some fashion in a relatively safe location, like at home.

That theory made some sense, but we might have been blowing smoke, for all we knew at the time. Still, there had to be some reason for her apparent lack of activity. She was either taking information out in her head, or we were missing the removal of hard materials, or she was no longer active. In any event, we certainly weren't gathering evidence of any active espionage in the absence of the FISA court order that would enable us to move a little closer to the target. We were frustrated.

At DIA, our end of the investigation entered a stage of near-listlessness. Mid-January passed, and no decision regarding Ana's assignment at the NIC was relayed to our level in the field. It seemed as though, with the pressure off, everyone had forgotten that the delay in her assignment to the NIC was only temporary. We hadn't actually fixed anything yet. I wondered whether anyone at CIA was actively pursuing a decision.

At the FBI, meanwhile, Steve was very busy, as were the agents on his squad. Steve had established teams of agents to support him, and those teams continued to prepare for the day when FISA authority would finally be granted. We conducted a walk-through of the DIAC for Steve's agents to familiarize them with the layout. Everything was all set, except the authority to activate those intrusive collection methods.

To the best of my knowledge, in fact, the FISA application hadn't reached the court yet. It was still bouncing around among, and between, the attorneys at FBI headquarters, the FBI headquarters staff supporting the investigation, and Steve, all of whom were tweaking the application to develop the best possible product for submission to the DOJ's Office of Intelligence Policy and Review (OIPR). The request would go to the FISA court only after OIPR approved it.

On January 18, 2001, one member of a congressional oversight committee was briefed on the Ana Montes investigation. That investigation was just one of many briefed to the committee that day. Two days later, George W. Bush was inaugurated as the forty-third president of the United States.

A few days after that, Ana's boyfriend Bill submitted to a routine counterintelligence scope polygraph examination administered by the Air Force. Bill had been indoctrinated into a sensitive DoD program, meaning he had received a formal briefing that included any special security measures for the program. Now he was required to successfully complete the examination before gaining access to program information or materials. His submission to a polygraph examination under the circumstances was entirely routine. Bill completed the exam with flying colors.

Gator and I were somewhat relieved by the news that Bill had successfully completed a polygraph examination. We had begun to suspect that Ana was either out of the espionage business altogether and therefore felt free to pursue a personal relationship with Bill, or that she was targeting Bill for future use as a witting or unwitting conduit for information that he alone could access for her. We reached no conclusions about the issue at that time, but we felt a little better about Bill, in any event.

On January 29, Ana Montes sent an e-mail to one of my co-workers in the security office, Linda Hatch. The e-mail informed Linda that Ana was no longer seeing a psychiatrist or counselor and that she was no longer taking medication to resolve her medical condition.

Ana's note was an interesting claim, in light of the fact that the FBI had established that she regularly filled her prescription and continued to see a counselor. With the completion of Bobby Speegle's investigation fast approaching, to be followed quickly by the polygraph examination, we surmised that Ana wanted to go on record as having no medication in her bloodstream during the examination. I considered asking a nurse to stand very visibly nearby during

Ana's polygraph, then suggesting that we were about to draw blood for a lab test, as though it was a recently enacted procedure for polygraph exams. But I never proposed it. Although it was nice to imagine, the last thing we wanted to do was to make Ana nervous.

The next day, January 30, Drew Winneberger and I traveled once again to the office of the DIA director, Admiral Wilson, at the Pentagon. We met members of DIA's Office of General Counsel in the admiral's outer office, and all of us trooped in to answer his questions. Wilson expressed his frustration with the slow pace of the investigation to date, and we similarly lamented the lack of FISA authority that might have provided greater insight into Ana's activities.

To make matters somewhat worse, our ploy to delay the National Intelligence Council assignment was running out of time. I recall that we were a rather glum and dispirited lot at that point in the investigation. Nothing seemed to be going our way.

Drew Winneberger met with a representative from CIA security a couple of days later regarding Ana's possible assignment to the NIC. It seemed unlikely that George Tenet would allow Ana to work at the NIC under the circumstances, but no firm decision had been passed down.

I could see the writing on the wall. We had to develop a scenario to finally derail the NIC assignment, and it would have to be done without raising the slightest suspicion on Ana's part. The latter seemed an impossibility. Ana was once again communicating directly with Fulton Armstrong, the NIO for Latin American affairs, and making plans for her upcoming assignment. Her management chain in the DIAC had already cut Ana's workload and transferred assignments and accounts to other analysts. Ana was as good as out the door. And I was desperate for ideas.

I discussed a couple of scenarios with Bobby Speegle that followed logically from his intelligence oversight investigation. Perhaps there was a lack of candor issue we could use. It appeared that Ana had attempted to manipulate DIA's Office of Public Affairs to contact the author of the *Soldier of Fortune* article without volunteering the fact that she had already done so. I suggested, in desperation, that we could blow that incident out of proportion. Bobby was obviously thinking more clearly than I was in those days, because he correctly pointed out that such a ploy would not hold water. We needed to think of something else.

Having drawn out the investigation as long as he could, Bobby had recently submitted his investigative report to the Office of General Counsel for review. I understood that that office had the option, if warranted, to refer the matter to the Office of the Assistant Secretary of Defense for Intelligence Oversight as a serious violation that was worthy of their review. I thought that we might parlay that review into a justification for the director of DIA to set aside Ana's appointment to the NIC. That suggestion fell flat, as well. It was time to look elsewhere for an idea.

I brainstormed with my counterintelligence analysts, Chris Simmons and John Kavanagh, and I desperately reached out to Reg Brown, as well. Reg had sensed our interest in Ana through a combination of our own carelessness (we had been asking for his opinions and guidance on a number of Ana-related issues lately) and his amazing ability to form a whole picture from the pieces of mosaic that we offered. After all, he was an analyst.

This time, we settled on a scenario to designate Ana as a "mission essential" analyst, someone whose knowledge, skills, and abilities were needed so urgently to accomplish a high-priority mission that DIA simply could not afford to let her go elsewhere, even temporarily. We decided to mount an operation to convince Ana and everyone in her chain of command that, owing to a series of events beyond everyone's control, she simply had to stay at DIA.

Once again, we wove real-world events into our scenario. The event this time was the implementation of Plan Colombia, the American effort to provide support to the government of Colombia in their war on drugs. The new Bush administration had made support for Plan Colombia a priority. Since Plan Colombia was implemented largely by the DoD's Southern Command, the success of Plan Colombia was a priority for the department. DIA would likely play a role in supporting the DoD's efforts in Plan Colombia. Now, all we had to do was to develop a role for Ana Montes that was so central, so important to DIA's support for Plan Colombia that we could not let her go to the NIC.

We needed an angle. Ana was a Cuba specialist, not a Colombia specialist. Fortunately, we had learned an interesting fact. After her many years on the Cuba account, Ana was currently slated to move to the Colombia account upon completion of her NIC fellowship. That fact gave us some wiggle room, but it wasn't enough to designate Ana Montes as "mission essential"—the only person who could do the job. Only that designation could justify the cancellation of her NIC assignment.

Once again, we had to spin a story that would be readily accepted not only by Ana Montes but also by everyone in her DIA chain of command and everyone at the NIC who expected her imminent transfer to Langley. To remain inside the bubble of ignorance, they all had to be fooled by our scenario.

Our difficulty was that Ana simply wasn't "mission essential" for Plan Colombia—unless we added a Cuba component. Ana was our Cuba expert, so Cuba had to be part of our scenario. Now, I did not know whether Cuba actually posed a threat to the success of Plan Colombia. I had no idea. But even a layman like me could imagine that the government of Cuba, which seems to oppose virtually every initiative taken by the United States in Latin America, not to mention other corners of the globe, might also oppose this effort in Colombia. Why not? It seemed plausible. And clearly, if Cuba posed a threat to the success of Plan Colombia, DIA could justify retaining Ana, its expert on Cuba, to support Plan Colombia. We could put the habeas-stoppus on her plans to leave the agency to work at the NIC.

All we needed now was some high-level concern about the possibility of a Cuban threat to the success of Plan Colombia. We needed someone at the right level to stand up and say, "Hey, wait a minute. Time out. What about the Cubans? Are they going to work against us in Colombia? Is this effort to assist Colombia going to be torpedoed by Fidel Castro? Somebody needs to look at this problem for us."

DIA's answer would be, "Let's put Ana Montes to work on that question. We'd better keep her here at DIA for a while. Cancel her assignment to the NIC." So we decided to manipulate the system. We planned to generate those kinds of questions at a high level and to create a demand for Ana Montes to remain at DIA. This was going to be fun.

Ordinarily, this is not the kind of operation that counterintelligence investigators develop, just to keep an investigation in play. It's difficult to implement and it's too complicated. It violates the KISS principle: Keep It Simple, Stupid. On the other hand, we were desperate, we were running out of time, and we were hamstrung by the requirement to keep Ana, her co-workers, her supervisors, and everyone at the NIC inside the bubble of ignorance of our investigation. Whatever we elected to do in our effort to keep Ana Montes at DIA and away from the NIC, it had to fool everyone, and it had to be done quickly. That's a tough assignment.

Reg Brown knew the system best, and he was instrumental to our success. Reg understood the culture, the process, and the flow of information throughout the process within which the analysts lived every day of their lives. Me? I had spent more than a decade working with and around DIA's analysts, but I was not one of them. My knowledge of their day-to-day working environment was limited. I had to defer to Reg's best judgment.

Reg believed that in order to succeed, the scenario required some real-world, real-time requests for priority support from the office of the chairman of the Joint Chiefs of Staff and from Southcom, specifically directed at DIA. Southcom and JCS would have to request a study of the potential negative impact upon the success of Plan Colombia by Cuba. Ana's management chain would then begin the process of building a priority by talking about the new emphasis. The director of DIA could announce from his lofty perch a need for seasoned analysts to work the problem immediately. Ana would have to stay at DIA. We had a week to accomplish this.

Reg got on the phone and called a colleague at JCS to discuss Plan Colombia. Then he wove into the conversation the possible threats to Plan Colombia that might be posed by various elements in the region: by Colombian insurgents, by Venezuela, and by Cuba. Finally, he suggested that a study of the problem might work to Southcom's benefit, and to JCS' benefit as well. All that was required, really, was a validated requirement submitted by JCS asking DIA to perform a study on the issue. Reg even offered to draft the requirement for JCS, and he did so. The draft requirement specifically tasked Ana's office to take the lead on the project, naming two additional DIA elements, including Reg's office, to collaborate on the project.

The requirement for a DIA study entered an automated tasking system the next day, and within hours it was being discussed at the highest levels of DIA's Directorate for Analysis and Production. Reg's fingerprints were nowhere to be seen. He then served as an action officer in support of the request, and he exploited that position to stir the pot among his fellow analysts on the new tasking, including Ana. I was amazed by the ease with which an individual could lead the intelligence community around by the nose. The most remarkable aspect of the entire thing was that the study actually had merit.

The real question, though, was whether the scenario was believable. No one could be left with so much as a nagging feeling that something was not right about this turn of events. I was also concerned that our scenario ultimately had to focus the spotlight on Ana, which could make her suspicious. At some point soon, we would have to ensure that Ana was selected to serve as *the* analyst to save the day for DIA on the suddenly elevated, high-priority requirement to study a Cuban question on Plan Colombia. We would be doing so at the last minute, just before she reported for duty with the NIC. The timing would be awfully coincidental, as she was foiled once again by circumstances in her attempt to get to the NIC.

This time the delay would come because she was so special—too special, in fact, to be released. Such a scenario would certainly feed her ego, but I feared that Ana would sense that something was wrong as soon as the spotlight conveniently fell upon her shoulders. If she went on alert, our case would effectively grind to a halt.

Still, something needed to happen. On February 7, I attended a meeting to discuss Ana's proposed assignment to the NIC and the options to derail it. The decision was announced to my level that day: Ana Montes would not be allowed to set foot inside the National Intelligence Council. How we prevented that from happening was our call.

Everyone turned to me. Only DIA could stop Ana from reporting to the NIC. Preferably, this would be accomplished without alerting her. It would be nice if we could cancel her polygraph examination, too, without letting her know that something unusual was happening behind the scenes. The logic behind that was simple. If Ana took and seemingly "passed" a polygraph test, as she had before, that would have to be reported to the FISA court. We didn't know how the court would view that circumstance, but it seemed best to avoid the issue altogether.

We had just a few days to accomplish all of the above. Any ideas?

I assured everyone that, indeed, I had a scenario in mind and that I had already launched Phase One. The relief on their faces was palpable. I briefed them on the particulars and all agreed that our scenario was sound. They wished me the best of luck and said they would stand by for the results. I can tell you that I wasted no time whatsoever in getting out of that room and back to my office. I had an awful lot to do.

On Tuesday, February 13, Drew Winneberger and I met again with Admiral Wilson and his deputy Mark Ewing at the Pentagon. The FISA authority had still not been issued. We were four months into the investigation and had nothing to show for it except our ulcers. At the meeting, I briefed the admiral on our Plan Colombia scenario to keep Ana Montes in place at DIA. I acknowledged up front that the scenario was weak. Wilson judged it even less kindly. He suspected that Ana would see right through the scenario and go on alert, and that any scenario that put the spotlight on her was doomed to the same outcome. He was right, of course. Ana was no fool.

Then he proposed an alternate scenario, just thinking out loud. Instead of focusing directly upon Ana, he suggested we do something that would cast a wider net and simply scoop Ana up along the way. Something that would not appear to be directed at her but would prevent her, nonetheless, from going to the NIC. He had that something in mind, and it revolved around the common practice of loaning analysts on a temporary basis from one agency to another within the intelligence community.

The very practice of sending DIA analysts to other agencies was one of the admiral's pet peeves. He saw lots of talent on the outbound track and very little brought back into our agency in return. We seemed to operate at a perpetual net loss through programs that enabled DIA analysts to spend their talent like currency at other agencies for weeks or months at a crack. Typically, as many as two hundred DIA employees were deployed to provide temporary support to other agencies at any one time. While our analysts were supporting other agencies, Admiral Wilson was placed in the uncomfortable position of having to respond to congressional complaints that DIA wasn't getting its work done, or that the agency was understaffed. He was tired of it.

So he proposed his scenario: an agency-wide freeze on all external analytical assignments. Just a temporary freeze, perhaps, while the agency studied the issue and attempted to develop a more equitable, manageable process for assigning analysts on a temporary basis to other agencies within the intelligence community. Exceptions could and would be granted—but not for Montes. She would have to stay at DIA.

The admiral's plan would effectively stop Ana from going to the NIC, but not without significant cost to DIA and the rest of the intelligence community. A proposal to cease cooperating with other members of the community on the routine exchange of analysts would generate discontent. First would come complaints at all levels, starting within DIA. Senior managers within the agency would have to quell the groundswell of grousing among analysts, who viewed the exchange program as a perk. Complaints would then filter into DIA from other member agencies of the intelligence community, each of which routinely loaned analysts to DIA under the exchange program and in turn depended upon DIA's expertise to accomplish its own mission. Finally, Congress would ask the admiral to account for the freeze. Admiral Wilson was willing to take that heat and to deal with it in order to advance the investigation into Ana Montes' activities on behalf of the Cuban government.

The deadline imposed by the completion of Bobby Speegle's investigation was fast approaching. It would be best to implement the agency-wide freeze right away. Waiting until the last minute would make it look a bit too coincidental in terms of Ana's departure for her NIC assignment.

But how to do it? A major announcement out of the blue would certainly seem suspicious. We didn't want anyone at the agency, particularly Ana, to wonder why the director chose that particular moment to halt the agency's participation in analytical exchanges. We needed a triggering event, an incident or event that would serve as a context for the announcement. Whatever we chose to do, it would have to clearly and convincingly explain the admiral's rationale for implementing a freeze, including the timing, all without any connection to Ana Montes.

The admiral had the perfect solution. He would throw a fit.

Ana Montes' senior portrait for her high school yearbook. She graduated in 1975 from Loch Raven High School, located just north of the city of Baltimore, Maryland. (Courtesy Baltimore County Public Schools)

Montes (second from right, middle row) poses with the members of the American Field Service chapter at Loch Raven High School. Ana's sister Lucy is second from left, middle row. Above the photo the yearbook reads: "The A.F.S. is an organization designed to foster mutual good will and understanding between nations…." (Courtesy Baltimore County Public Schools)

DIA analyst Montes, principal U.S. analyst for El Salvador and Nicaragua, visiting U.S. Army bases in El Salvador during a spring 1987 orientation tour. A few weeks after Montes visited his base, U.S. Army Special Forces Staff Sergeant Gregory A. Fronius was killed by Cuba-backed guerrillas. (Defense Department photo)

A casual shot of Montes from the 1975 yearbook. (Courtesy Baltimore County Public Schools)

Staff Sgt. Gregory A. Fronius, U.S. Army Special Forces, just before leaving for El Salvador in 1986. (U.S. Army photo)

Greg Fronius training an indigenous soldier. (Courtesy of Celinda Carney)

Cemetery marker for Greg Fronius. (Courtesy of Celinda Carney)

U.S. Army Certificate of Achievement awarded to Montes in December 1989 for her support to the human intelligence operation in El Salvador. (Defense Department photo).

Montes receiving an award from then-DIA director Lt. Gen. Harry E. Soyster, U.S. Army. (DIA photo)

Marty Scheina, who hired Montes at DIA in 1985 and was still her supervisor when she was arrested, awards Montes a DIA Special Achievement Award. (DIA photo)

In 1997, then-Director of Central Intelligence George J. Tenet gives Montes a Certificate of Distinction, the third highest national-level intelligence award. (Office of the Director of Central Intelligence photo)

Ana Montes' condominium building in Cleveland Park, near the National Zoo in Washington, D.C. Montes placed her antennae close to the window of her corner unit to receive coded messages from Havana three nights per week. (DIA photo)

Montes (front, in white) assumes her characteristic assertive posture in a meeting at DIA. (DIA photo)

Ana celebrates a birthday in her DIA cubicle, on a wall of which is a map of Cuba. (DIA photo)

Contrary to a perception that Montes was cold and distant, Montes shows a lighter side with military officers at DIA. (DIA photo)

Montes caught in a rare casual moment by her boyfriend during their summer 2001 vacation in Miami. (DIA photo)

Montes' mug shot after her arrest on the morning of September 21, 2001. (Justice Department photo)

12

THE FREEZE

AFTER THE MEETING WITH ADMIRAL WILSON, Drew Winneberger and I drove from the Pentagon to the DIAC on Bolling Air Force Base. Our objective was to brief Ana's senior manager, Caryne Wagner. Until that point, Caryne was inside Ana's bubble, completely unaware of our investigation. Now we needed her assistance to execute the freeze.

Caryne was surprised and concerned to learn about the investigation, but she accepted our briefing instantly and turned immediately to how she could help us. On hearing the plan, however, she questioned how she could handle the flood of complaints that would naturally flow from analysts to first-line supervisors and then to her office after a freeze was announced. She did not deal with the nuts and bolts management of day-to-day operational affairs within the DI. That function was left to her deputy, Dave Curtin. So her bottom line was simple: Dave had to join the team.

That was a big step, and risky. Dave had known and worked with Ana for approximately a decade. Less than two years earlier, while serving as Ana's second-level supervisor, he had engineered her special EIP promotion to the GS-14 level. Professionally, he thought the world of her, putting him near the top of our list of people whom we wished to avoid during the Ana Montes investigation. Learning that his star analyst was actually a spy would be a huge shock, making it difficult for him to maintain a "business as usual" attitude toward her. Still, Caryne was correct: Only Dave could run interference for her by handling Ana's supervisors. We agreed to brief him as soon as possible.

On Valentine's Day, February 14, Ana departed for Miami to spend a week with her boyfriend Bill. A couple of days later, a judge on the FISA court authorized the use of intrusive techniques to collect information about Ana's activities. The FBI swung into high gear, and our advance preparations began to pay off as systems went into place to actively monitor Ana Montes around the clock. We waited hungrily for her return from Miami.

So far the investigation had produced very little. The FBI had developed one additional, though key, piece of corroborating evidence that matched Ana Montes against another data point. But that was all of the additional evidence that we had gathered in four months. There's only so much that can be accomplished through a review of records and physical surveillance.

On February 21, Drew Winneberger and I traveled to the DIAC again, this time to brief Dave Curtin on the case. I laid the case out for him piece by piece. He was devastated. But by the end of the briefing, he seemed even more convinced than I was that Ana Montes was a spy.

The broad implications of her activities on behalf of the Cubans could be fully appreciated only by intelligence professionals like Dave. The rest of us, laymen by comparison, are capable of grasping only a vague and superficial understanding of the damage that Ana Montes caused our nation. Dave also took the depth of Ana's betrayal personally. I am certain that it bothers him to this day. He was one of several senior members of the U.S. intelligence community who thought the world of Ana Montes as an analyst. Dave had gone out of his way to ensure that she enjoyed opportunities for advancement and opportunities to broaden her experience and value to the intelligence community. Dave was simply devastated.

He agreed to play a key role in the admiral's scenario. The managers in Ana's chain of command would raise Cain about the freeze, but he was determined to do his part in support of the investigation, however painful it might be for him personally.

Another week passed before we could advance the admiral's scenario. On Wednesday, February 28, Admiral Wilson hosted a meeting in his Pentagon office that was attended by some pretty heavy hitters at DIA, including his deputy, Mark Ewing, his military aide, Capt. Joseph Stewart, Caryne Wagner, and Dave Curtin. Drew and I completed the list of attendees. The purpose of the meeting was essentially to establish the mechanics of the admiral's scenario, including the timetable.

This time, the mechanics were fairly simple. Caryne would feed a "meatball" to the admiral during a weekly video teleconference meeting with senior DIA managers. The meatball would be an off-hand comment to the effect that DI was unable to meet some specific requirement because key analysts were on assignment to another agency. The admiral would then throw his fit, and everyone who participated in the video-teleconference would be on notice that some kind of change was in the offing. It would then be up to Mark Ewing to announce the freeze of external assignments and up to Dave to ensure that Ana's was among them.

After listening to Admiral Wilson that day, I believed the plan would work. He launched into a tirade about external analytical assignments and the ill effect that those assignments had visited upon his agency. It truly did make him angry. I must admit I found it somewhat amusing to listen to him as he railed on about a topic that I found to be abstract and generally inconsequential. I can tell you this, though: It really upset him.

The senior executives were prepared to launch Admiral Wilson's scenario the next morning. Our meeting broke up, and I observed to Drew that it was Ana Montes' birthday. She turned forty-four that day. We were preparing quite a birthday present for her. Her agency's senior managers were pulling strings behind the scenes in an effort to ensure that her forty-fifth year was spent in prison.

Bill surprised Ana by showing up in Washington on her birthday. He would remain in town through the weekend. If our scenario worked, it would be a week of surprises.

The admiral's tantrum went off according to plan. He commented during the next morning's video-teleconference with senior DIA managers that Plan Colombia seemed to be heating up. He then casually asked Caryne Wagner, who "owned" the analytical assets at DIA, how she planned to address the issue and whether she was sufficiently staffed to do so. Caryne delivered the meatball. DI, she responded, had several initiatives under way to address the issue, but unfortunately, some of her best analysts were temporarily assigned to joint task forces or other external assignments, and she was experiencing some difficulty drawing from internal resources to meet the requirement. She would do her best. That was the admiral's cue.

They got an earful, and it was all from the heart. Admiral Wilson did not have to fake his hissy fit; it was real. There must have been no doubt in the minds of the admiral's senior managers but that something was about to be done about the agency's "problem" with external analyst assignments. By the end of the day, rumors about the admiral's performance had filtered down from his senior managers to the rank-and-file analysts in the agency.

Mark Ewing's role as deputy director of DIA was to serve as Admiral Wilson's action officer. On Friday morning, March 1, he sent an e-mail to DIA's senior managers, including Caryne Wagner. His e-mail mentioned the admiral's concerns about external analytical assignments and announced an immediate, temporary freeze on those assignments until a proper study of the problem could be completed. Caryne forwarded the e-mail to Dave, with an instruction to put it into effect. Dave was now the key player in our effort to freeze Ana Montes at DIA.

Dave first forwarded the e-mail to his own senior management staff and then followed up with a telephonic summons to each of his managers to attend a meeting in his office that morning. Dave understood his managers, and he understood the culture at DIA. His managers would salute the admiral's order smartly and feign compliance, but they would work behind the scenes to secure exceptions to the new rule for their favorite employees. Ana was one of them.

Fortunately, Dave was a master of the bureaucratic game and was able to anticipate every move that his managers were likely to make on Ana's behalf. He wished to deal with those maneuvers as directly as possible, without drawing any direct attention to Ana. During the meeting, he announced that exceptions to the new policy would be accepted on a case-by-case basis. Given the fervency of the director's feelings on the issue, however, they couldn't expect much in the way of grace. Dave asked his managers to compile lists of the analysts who would be affected by the freeze and to e-mail those lists to him before the end of the day.

As Dave had suspected, the list from Ana's direct chain of supervisors did not include her name. Her immediate supervisors had probably omitted her name intentionally in an effort to slip her past the freeze because she had already been selected and processed for the NIC assignment. She practically had one foot out the door already. Dave was ready for them. A quick phone call to her third-level supervisor did the trick. Ana's name was back on the list, and she was frozen.

Montes' immediate chain of supervisors assured Ana that they would obtain an exception to the freeze on her behalf. They submitted a request for such a waiver, but of course the request was denied after careful review by DIA's senior managers. The fix was in.

Nevertheless, the bureaucracy continued to work in support of Ana Montes. Fulton Armstrong and his subordinates at the National Intelligence Council also worked from their end of the analyst exchange pipeline to obtain a waiver for Ana. We were confident that the director and deputy director of DIA could withstand any attempt by the NIC staff to obtain a waiver. Still, their continued efforts gave Ana some reason to hope that her assignment to the NIC might occur after all, despite the freeze. As you'll see, that flicker of hope nearly cost us dearly.

Shortly after Mark Ewing's e-mail was transmitted to senior managers that Friday morning, I participated in a meeting at FBI headquarters. I briefed those present on the status of the admiral's scenario and assured them that we had the situation under control and could now proceed with the investigation.

Everything was clicking along for us. The full field investigation had been granted, the FBI had developed some good information that enabled the Department of Justice to obtain FISA authority for the use of intrusive intelligence collection techniques, and now we had fixed Ana Montes in place at DIA. George Tenet would be pleased to know that DIA had kept Ana away from his National Intelligence Council. And as far as we knew, Ana was ignorant of our activities behind the scenes. She remained inside the bubble.

There remained only one bump in the road: Ana's polygraph appointment. Upon learning from Bobby Speegle that his investigation was complete, Ana contacted our polygraph team to request again that they schedule her for a polygraph so that she could zip up to the NIC as soon as possible. She was clearly still hoping that a way could still be found to release her from the agency-wide freeze. We fudged things a bit in order to buy additional time, but Ana's polygraph was scheduled for March 14, less than two weeks away.

This was a potential problem. FISA warrants that authorize the use of certain types of investigative techniques are good for only ninety days. After that, the FBI and Justice Department must renew the warrants to continue using those very intrusive investigative techniques against a suspect. The renewal affidavit must include a summary of pertinent information developed through investigation since the preceding warrant was issued. If Ana did well on the DIA polygraph exam, as she had in the past, those results would have to be included.

Once again, it seemed best to avoid the issue altogether. In other words: No polygraph examination for Ana Montes. That was not so easily accomplished if the goal was to cancel the appointment without alerting her. We couldn't risk putting Ana on alert by asking the DIA polygraph team to contact her out of the blue, unexpectedly and without explanation, to cancel the polygraph appointment.

But I had a plan. I suspected that Ana would do us all a favor by canceling her own appointment with the polygraph team, if only we gave her enough time to do so. I didn't volunteer that thought to anyone but Gator, however. I kept my counsel and merely offered assurances to everyone else that DIA would work to develop some means to cancel Ana's polygraph appointment. I doubted they would accept my belief that the best course of action was to simply sit tight, do nothing, and allow Ana to cancel the polygraph appointment by herself.

My rationale was simple: Ana Montes was still the same person. When offered an opportunity to avoid a polygraph examination during her conversation with Bobby Speegle back in December, she had jumped at the chance to do so. I believed that she would do it again. She had only to realize that, since she wasn't going to the NIC assignment after all, there was no need for her to take a polygraph test.

On Thursday, March 8, someone way above my pay grade called to discuss my efforts to cancel Ana's polygraph examination. The polygraph appointment was less than a week away, and he was worried. Ana's polygraph was scheduled for the following Wednesday. I told him we were still working on it, but in fact I was just buying time.

On Monday, I received yet another call from another person at a high level. At the news that Ana's polygraph had not yet been canceled, my caller all but accused me of deliberately sabotaging the investigation by failing to take actions to cancel the polygraph appointment. By then, even I was beginning to sweat. If Ana submitted to our polygraph examination and inexplicably passed it, my superiors would have me for lunch.

My caller was taking notes on our conversation. Finally, she summarized our exchange rather sarcastically, "So, let me see if I understand you correctly. Your plan is to wait and do nothing. And you're hoping that Ana Montes is going to pick up the phone to cancel her own appointment, is that right?"

Well, yes.

At nine o'clock on Tuesday morning, the day before the scheduled exam, Gator and I participated in a meeting with our polygraph team, including Harry Pittman, who served as DIA's polygraph team leader, my boss Jerry Craig, who was responsible for both the polygraph team and the investigations team of which I was a member, and Dave Cameron, the designated examiner. At this stage of the game, we were resigned to the fact that the polygraph of Ana Montes was going to occur as scheduled and that we would have to simply deal with the results of that polygraph, come what may. We understood that the investigation of Ana would continue, regardless of the examination results, and abiding by any decisions by the FISA court that might stem in part from those results. We had to play the cards that were dealt.

It was ten o'clock, and we'd been meeting for an hour. As we gathered our things to leave, a distinctive bell alerted everyone present to the receipt on Jerry's personal computer of an e-mail from within the agency. It was from Montes. And you should have seen the look on Jerry Craig's face when he announced that Ana was inquiring whether she really needed to take a polygraph test in light of the fact that her assignment to the NIC had been indefinitely postponed.

Needless to say, we accommodated her request to cancel the polygraph.

13

SUSPICIOUS ACTIVITY

WITH THE SUCCESSFUL EFFORT TO DERAIL Ana Montes' assignment to the National Intelligence Council and the cancellation of her polygraph examination, the change in our attitudes was palpable. Ana was firmly in place at DIA, apparently not on alert, and we had all systems up and running to monitor her activities very closely around the clock.

The FBI's physical surveillance had been underway for months by March 2001. The team had established a good baseline for Ana's normal, routine behavior. Now they were looking for anything out of the ordinary that might suggest she was engaged in some kind of clandestine contact with the Cubans. Nothing of consequence had been detected to date. Ana's polygraph had been scheduled for Wednesday, March 14, 2001, but we had obligingly canceled the exam upon receipt of her e-mail in Jerry Craig's office the previous day. March 14, then, was just another day at the office for Ana Montes.

But March 14 was anything but just another day for many of us, as Vice President Dick Cheney, Secretary of Defense Donald Rumsfeld, and Director of Central Intelligence George Tenet visited the DIAC. It was a combined courtesy call and orientation tour for the new vice president and secretary of defense, and as you might imagine, there was a lot of brass inside the building that day. Lots of security, too. Inside our DIAC command post, not far from

Ana's cubicle, we kept close tabs on her activity. To the best of our knowledge, she took no special interest in our visitors.

Weeks passed, and still we observed nothing out of the ordinary in Ana's behavior—nothing to suggest that she was actively engaged in espionage. Her typical work day ran from eight o'clock in the morning to five o'clock in the afternoon. You could almost set your watch by her. She was very punctual. And Ana had her nose squarely on the grindstone, all day long. I mean, the woman did not stop to take a breath. She worked continuously, throughout the day. At eight o'clock in the morning, Ana would walk directly to her cubicle on the sixth floor of the DIAC, and without a pause she would turn her computer on and wade directly into her workload. No time was wasted waiting for the coffee to perk. No stopping for a doughnut in the cafeteria. No chit-chat with her co-workers. Just work. It was as though she'd think about work during the commute to the office, and when she arrived, she simply dove into it.

She'd work straight through to lunchtime, nonstop, and it wasn't busywork. On the contrary, she was very efficient. The woman simply gobbled up the workload. For lunch, Ana would typically go downstairs to the cafeteria, toss a salad or a bowl of soup onto her tray, and take it back to her cubicle, alone. She worked through lunch virtually every day, in her cubicle, at her desk, with her computer keyboard at hand. At five o'clock— sometimes at four-thirty—she'd go home. She almost never worked later than five during the normal workweek and almost never went into work on a Saturday or a Sunday.

On a typical evening after work, Ana performed personal errands as most of us do, shopping for fresh vegetables and other foods for dinner. She ate sparingly, and only food that was good for her. She might stop by the local pharmacy or pop into the dry cleaning shop on the corner. Afterward, she'd head for home, a condo in Washington's Cleveland Park district, near the National Zoo. Once she got there, she usually stayed put, rarely venturing out at night. She was a homebody, and she kept her place tidy and neat. Several times per week she worked out at the gym for a couple of hours, perhaps to relieve the stress of living a double life. She attended Mass regularly, rarely missing a service.

And she was a reader. Ana's library at home was filled with volumes of history and of political studies of Latin America, as you might expect of a Latin America specialist. Fidel Castro and Che Guevara, Castro's late comrade who supported armed resistance to capitalism throughout Central and South America, figured quite prominently on her shelves.

I was certain that I had matched the right person against the FBI's UNSUB data points. But even I was beginning to doubt that Ana Montes was still active. There were times when I wished I could simply will her to remove some classified material from the DIAC, but we did not observe her doing so.

Bill arrived in Washington in time for Easter. He was scheduled to attend a three-week training session at DIA, of all places, and his classes were right there in the DIAC, just a short walk from our DIAC command post. On May 16, we learned that Bill had accepted a new job within the DoD. He hoped to report for his new assignment by the end of the summer, some time after DIA adjudicated his security clearance to ensure that he met the personnel security standards for his new billet. Gator and I would be reviewing the nomination package forwarded to DIA for Bill's security clearance. And so life continued on, frustratingly uneventful.

That Sunday, May 20, 2001, Ana followed her normal routine of attending Mass then going shopping in the afternoon. She patronized a Hecht's store on Wisconsin Avenue in Chevy Chase, Maryland. Members of the surveillance team had seen her enter that particular store many times in the past. In fact, she went there almost every Sunday, except when she had other appointments or when Bill was in town. As usual, she parked her car on the top deck of a parking garage next to Hecht's then walked from her car into the store.

A short while later, Ana exited the store at the lower level and sat down on a half-wall located next to two public telephones. She glanced at her watch, and at exactly 1:30 PM she placed a short call from one of the telephones that lasted perhaps a minute. She then walked to her car and left the area. Members of the surveillance team took note of the call, suspecting it was for operational purposes. They knew Ana carried a cell phone wherever she went. She had it with her when she placed the call from the public telephone near Hecht's. There was something odd about that call.

Ana then drove south on Wisconsin Avenue, seemingly headed back home. Unexpectedly, however, she parked her car on the street then doubled back on foot in the opposite direction, walking north along Wisconsin Avenue for a couple of blocks. As she did so, she passed a public telephone booth that appeared to be in good operating order.

Next she crossed Wisconsin Avenue and entered a sporting goods store at the end of the block, spent a few minutes inside, then emerged with a shopping bag in one hand as though she had just purchased an item. In Washington's Northwest section, Wisconsin Avenue is a wide, busy street with two lanes of traffic in each direction. Those doing the surveillance thought the fact Ana chose to cross such a major street suggested she had a specific destination in mind. After leaving the sporting goods store, Ana walked to a nearby public telephone booth. At exactly 2:00 PM she placed another brief call from the public phone. She then walked back to her car and drove home.

14

A LONG SUMMER

FBI AGENTS AND THEIR CO-WORKERS in Miami likely participated in a low-key celebration on June 8, 2001. Convicted members of the Cuban Wasp network received their prison sentences that day. Their sentencing was the culmination of more than five years of effort by the FBI and the Justice Department, and I imagined that Ana's sister was among those at the FBI who joined in celebration of the victory over Cuban intelligence. She could rightly feel proud and happy about her contribution to the operation's success. Ana, by contrast, might well have spent June 8 in fear that she might someday share the Wasp network's fate at the hands of the FBI. Ana and her sister, it seemed, had never been so far apart.

Fortunately, Bill came to town shortly after June 8. He was scheduled to participate in an interagency study on the intelligence community's collection efforts against Cuba, and he would be in Washington for about two weeks. Bill's visit occurred at just the right moment. Ana needed the company and emotional support after the announced sentences of the Wasp network. Though she couldn't share her concerns with Bill, his presence would serve as a much-needed distraction for her troubled mind.

Throughout much of the spring, Ana participated in developing a national intelligence estimate (NIE) on Cuba. NIEs are intelligence community assessments that greatly impact the formulation of U.S. foreign policy. As the queen of Cuba—the top U.S. Cuba analyst in the community—Ana was in a position to greatly influence U.S. foreign policy.

In the late spring and through June, she worked to update the intelligence community assessment (ICA) of the Cuban armed forces, a document that would serve as a basis for contingency planning for military engagements with Cuba. An ICA is the intelligence community's way of saying to the country's warfighters, "This is what you're up against. This is what the Cuban military is capable of doing, and this is what they are likely to do in any given situation." The assessment goes into great detail.

Fidel Castro's mole was writing the intelligence community's assessment of Cuba for use by U.S. war planners. This was not low-level stuff. To put it another way, a Cuban agent was spending her summer shaping the U.S. military's approach toward Cuba in the event a crisis developed between the two nations.

It was true that others above Ana's station, such as Fulton Armstrong, the NIO for Latin American affairs, might review her assessment and provide input to ensure her key judgments reflected those of the broader intelligence community, but those judgments were largely her own. Besides, those senior reviewers knew and respected her work. If we hadn't derailed her assignment, she would have been working with Armstrong at that moment as part of her research fellowship. It was Ana Montes, the intelligence community's premier expert on Cuban political and military affairs, who developed the basic analysis behind those "broader intelligence community" judgments for the NIE and the ICA in the first place. That's why Ana was tasked to draft both documents.

The fact that Montes was so heavily involved in the process of establishing U.S. foreign policy and military doctrine weighed heavily on Admiral Wilson's mind throughout the summer. Ultimately, he was responsible for the decision to leave her in place, with access to the nation's innermost secrets, while the FBI's investigation plowed ahead. He felt justified in that decision as long as the investigation showed progress. Still, the admiral was constantly aware of his responsibility to balance the need to protect our national security against the needs of the FBI for more time to complete its investigation. It was a weighty responsibility that he bore alone. As DIA director, he could terminate Ana's continued access to sensitive information whenever he felt it necessary. But removing that access would almost certainly alarm Ana and reduce the likelihood that the FBI would be able to gather sufficient evidence to support a prosecution of her in federal court. The admiral stood in the middle, like a fulcrum balancing two options.

In the meantime, pressure built steadily throughout the summer to lift DIA's ban on external analyst assignments—the policy that had the secret objective of freezing Ana in place at DIA. We met again with Admiral Wilson and his deputy director Mark Ewing to discuss our options. Internal pressure from DIA analysts was manageable, but external pressure from the rest of the intelligence community was rising. Ewing foresaw a need to lift the freeze by the end of the summer. We would have to develop a Plan B to keep Ana at DIA.

My wife and I had long planned to take a vacation with our kids in July 2001. We drove down to Disney World for a few days and then boarded the *Disney Magic* for a cruise into the Caribbean. Coincidentally, Ana and Bill planned to take a vacation at about the same time, traveling first to Miami and then to Puerto Rico for a Montes family reunion—another indication of their growing intimacy. The *Disney Magic* sailed within eighteen miles of the Puerto Rican shoreline on the evening of July 8. I stood on our balcony peering into the distance and wondering whether Ana sensed my presence at that moment. It seemed that I could not get away from this woman even while on vacation.

Soon after my return to the office, the lack of progress in our investigation prompted Admiral Wilson to call a meeting on July 19. He called for an extensive search of Ana's residence under authority of the FISA warrant as soon as practicable in order to move things along. The admiral was a patient man, but his patience had limits.

The search warrant was open-ended, but there was something special we were looking for. Earlier, I mentioned the possibility that Ana might be taking information out of the DIA in her head then writing it down elsewhere—most likely at home—and encoding it for delivery or transmission. If she was still an active spy, that theory explained why no physical materials were leaving the building. It also suggested that she was likely to have an encryption/decryption system hidden away—again, most likely at home.

If Ana was passing on coded information, we also thought we knew how. Despite owning a cell phone, she had continued to make use of a variety of public pay phones. The FBI team had learned that these calls were directed to pagers in New York City. Our assumption was that she was punching in numeric codes during the phone calls, which her Cuban handlers could pick up and decode from the pagers. We needed to find that encryption/decryption system. (Her handlers also sent coded messages in the other direction, from themselves to Ana, but they used a different method for those. We eventually learned that she received the messages on a shortwave radio.)

The problem with searching Ana's condo was that it had to be done discreetly. Needless to say, we didn't want to let Ana or any of her neighbors know that something was going on. To search an entire residence both thoroughly and surreptitiously, we simply had to get Ana out of town for at least a full day, if not longer.

Ana's next scheduled business trip outside the Washington area was a trip to Miami in September 2001. Even that date, we knew, was not set in cement. It could slip or be canceled altogether. Besides, September was too far off. We needed her to take an official trip sometime soon, preferably in August. Dave Curtin was the only person who could make this happen, so I tapped into him for the second time in the investigation. He didn't disappoint me.

DIA has a facility in Huntsville, Alabama, called the Missiles and Space Intelligence Center (MSIC). Located on the Redstone Arsenal near the Marshall Space Flight Center, MSIC is staffed, like the DIAC, with DIA analysts. Dave had just returned from a business trip to MSIC, so he chose it as the site for Ana's business trip.

Ana wouldn't be going alone. Dave organized a high-priority, short-fuse conference on an issue that would require a broad spectrum of expertise. Only the most senior and experienced analysts from DIA were chosen to participate in the conference, all hand-picked by Dave. Dave threw his conference together in just a couple of days.

Ana's supervisors, however, had other plans. As it turned out, Ana didn't really want to go to the conference. She understood the need for a conference to iron out some longstanding problems between MSIC analysts and DIAC analysts, but she didn't understand the choice of venues. MSIC was about a thousand miles south of Washington, and the very thought of traveling that far for a two-day conference seemed a poor use of her time. Her supervisors substituted the name of another analyst on their list of participants, omitting Ana's name altogether, and attempted to slip the list past a busy Dave Curtin while giving their prize analyst a break.

They should have known better. Dave had a habit of getting into work early to read his e-mails and clear his desk of administrative matters before launching into his day. I caught Dave on the way out of the DIAC at about six-thirty the next morning as I was on my way into work. He told me about the attempt by Montes' supervisors to torpedo his plan and about his own response. That was Dave at his bureaucratic best.

Fortunately, another analytical unit under Dave's purview had attempted the same trick. Dave shot a response back down the supervisory chain, scorching every recalcitrant manager in turn. He didn't have time for their games. These people were on his list for a purpose. Each offered something unique and necessary for the conference and had been hand-picked. Then Dave articulated his rationale for having selected both Ana and the other analyst and he wrote that he would see them all on the plane. End of story.

I loved it, for several reasons. First, because Dave's response was certain to get Ana out of town, as we desired. Second, because word of Dave's response was bound to filter down to Ana, and it would appeal to her ego. It would make her feel special and important—so important that her own ego would quell any suspicions that might otherwise have arisen about the sudden departure from Washington for a distant locale. Finally, I loved it because he handled the turn of events by himself. He simply knew what needed to be done, and he did it. I like that.

Sure enough, a team of twenty analysts left Washington for the conference in Huntsville, Alabama, on Tuesday evening, August 7. Ana Montes was among them. But our efforts were for naught. Every investigative action taken during Ana's absence failed to produce more evidence of operational activity on behalf of the Cuban Intelligence Service. If she had crypto materials—or any other incriminating possessions—apparently she hadn't left them behind when she went on the trip.

This lack of results was truly a crushing blow. The admiral had spent much of the summer reminding us of the need to show progress in the investigation. We risked additional damage to national security by allowing Ana to continue her employment at DIA, and he could justify keeping her on the payroll only as long as the FBI's efforts showed significant progress. The admiral would not be amused by this setback.

Sure enough, Admiral Wilson called a meeting the day after the search. We believed we had enough evidence against Ana to terminate her employment at the agency. Whether the Justice Department felt it had sufficient evidence to support charges that she had violated federal statutes as well was another issue, and not our own. Everyone understood that Ana could not be allowed to continue her access to classified information forever. The FBI had had its shot.

Meanwhile, internal and external pressure against the admiral's freeze on external analytical assignments was nearing the breaking point. It might be time to close this thing down.

Wilson decided to schedule a meeting with the FBI to discuss the end game for their investigation. A meeting was set for August 20. We were beside ourselves with frustration. Ana simply had to have that encryption/decryption system somewhere close by.

The next day, Friday, August 10, FBI headquarters hosted a retirement party for Terry Holstead, one of the senior managers involved in the Ana Montes investigation. Terry had put in more than thirty years with the bureau, and quite a crowd turned out to celebrate his transition to retirement. Gator and I were among them. Someone commented that Terry's true forte with the FBI had been his ability to forge bonds with outside agencies. I had to agree that Terry had forged a bond with DIA and earned my respect as he worked to keep the investigation on track. I smile now, imagining that Terry was fishing in some trout stream out West the day that Ana was finally arrested. And happy to be there.

It was around that time that our thoughts turned to Ana's tote bag. She carried it wherever she went, and she never seemed to leave it anywhere. Perhaps the crypto materials were inside the bag. Maybe she carried those materials into work every day to keep them close and safe. We needed to get close enough to search that bag.

Getting to the tote bag while Montes was outside of work was impossible. She practically slept with the thing. We needed a plan to get to it while she was at work, inside the DIAC.

15

BORROWING THE LADY'S PURSE

THERE WAS VERY LITTLE TIME LEFT. Admiral Wilson's meeting with the FBI was scheduled for Monday, August 20. That left us just over one week—or five full workdays, Monday to Friday—to devise a means to search Ana's tote bag while she was at work then successfully execute the plan. I was the DIA action officer, so responsibility for developing the plan fell to me.

Back in my high school algebra class, I learned a valuable problem-solving strategy. To solve a seemingly complex problem, it's best to break the problem down into its component parts. Solve each part, and you've solved the problem. That was the approach I took to borrowing Ana's tote bag.

The difficulty lay in not getting caught. Ana shared a large cubicle with one other analyst in an open-bay workspace of similar cubicles. The cubicles were occupied throughout the day by Ana's co-workers, the people with whom Ana had worked for many years. They formed their own little village, of sorts, in a corner on the sixth floor of the DIAC. Like the occupants of any village, Ana and her co-workers had settled into a comfortable routine of daily life. They were used to one another, used to the ebb and flow of activity around them, and quick to note the introduction of anything out of the ordinary—like strangers.

Now I broke down the problem into its component parts. I had to introduce one or more strangers to the village, have one of them take Montes' tote bag and remove it from her cubicle, retain it long enough for a thorough search, and return it to its original spot in her cubicle, all without Ana's knowledge, without alerting her cubicle mate, and without raising an eyebrow among her co-workers. To complicate matters, Ana rarely left her cubicle for more than a few minutes at any time during the day, and she was never observed to leave the tote bag in her cubicle during a prolonged absence.

It took me about fifteen minutes to develop my plan. I spent the rest of my day on Friday making necessary arrangements.

On Monday, August 13, Drew Winneberger briefed Admiral Wilson on the plan. The admiral understood that this was an effort to find the crypto material that had eluded us during the prolonged search of Ana's residence. But he also understood it was risky. If we were caught—if anyone raised an alarm— the entire investigation could come to a crashing halt. Ana would go on alert, and we might as well close the case. With the admiral's meeting with the FBI so few days away, however, that risk was worth taking. We planned to execute our operation Thursday morning.

I spent most of Monday making contacts within the agency, briefing necessary participants on their roles within the plan and securing their commitments. That afternoon, I took my oldest son to the doctor. He'd suffered an injury during football practice and, you know, one cannot stop being a dad, even while planning to steal a lady's purse.

Tuesday was a disaster. I spent the better part of my day at home, waiting for an air-conditioning repairman to rescue my family from the heat of the Washington summer. The brake light on our van was beginning to fail as well, and I was just waiting for something else to go wrong. Bad luck, they say, comes in threes. I just wanted my bad luck to expend itself that day.

The next morning, Ana deviated from her usual route to work to place a call from a public telephone to a pager based in New York City. She was communicating with her Cuban handlers again. I spent the day double-checking everything and everyone for the next day's event. We were ready.

Thursday morning, Ana parked in her usual spot in a parking lot across the street from the DIAC. She dropped some mail off at a post office box beside the parking lot then walked into work. A member of the surveillance team took note of her use of the mailbox. In doing so, he paused just long enough to catch the eye of an alert Bolling Air Force Base policeman, who suspected something unusual was going on. He was right. Ana Montes continued to walk in blissful ignorance toward the DIAC, but the surveillance team member found himself in the embarrassing position of having to explain his rather suspicious conduct to a cop who was just doing his job. Score one point for the base police.

I met with three members of the purse-snatching team in a staging room on the sixth floor of the DIAC about eight-thirty that morning. Two technicians joined us shortly thereafter, including one who was prepared to operate a portable X-ray device, if needed. That made six of us crammed together inside a very small workspace. Another arrival, Lt. Carl Schweitzer of DIA's police force, squeezed into the room, followed by one more technician, Josh Mosley, a Navy enlisted man whose specialty was "comms." Josh worked with fiber optics and other communication equipment. He would be playing the "computer guy." Everyone seemed ready to roll.

Like the components of the problem, the components of our plan seemed simple and straightforward enough. The first was to remove Ana from the area and keep her under control for a sufficient period of time to accomplish the search of her tote bag. The second was to encourage her to leave her tote bag behind while she was engaged elsewhere. The third was to remove her unsuspecting cubicle mate from the area and keep him under control for a sufficient period of time to accomplish the search. The final component was to distract Ana's co-workers and introduce two strangers among them without causing undue alarm. Here's how it worked.

Dave Curtin had set the stage for me the previous Friday by sending an e-mail to about twenty DIA analysts, inviting them to a meeting scheduled for nine o'clock that morning. The purpose of the meeting was ostensibly to discuss the status of DIA's response to an event that had occurred just a week or so earlier. The event involved Venezuelan-U.S. relations, but it had broader implications for the region as well, particularly for Venezuela's neighbor Colombia. Fortunately for us, Cuba played a role, too. This was not a fabricated event. It actually occurred. Each of the experts whom Dave called upon to attend his meeting was fully aware of it, and Ana was among them.

We decided to hold the meeting in a conference room on the seventh floor of the DIAC, just a short walk down a corridor and up the stairs from Ana's cubicle. That made the meeting convenient for her, and we surmised that she might feel comfortable leaving her tote bag behind if the meeting were held just a short distance from her cubicle. The meeting site was within her comfort zone.

Through Dave, we also gave Ana some responsibility to brief attendees on the Cuban piece of the issue in question. By assigning her that role, we ensured that she would view the meeting with some seriousness. This was business—her business—and Ana was a featured speaker. She might be expected to bring some notes and a notebook to such a meeting, but not something as unprofessional as a tote bag. We hoped that she would feel inclined to leave it behind.

We decided, too, to start the meeting at nine o'clock with a view toward concluding the meeting at ten-thirty. Ana usually arrived at work by eight o'clock, and she habitually placed her tote bag on a corner of her desk. We wanted to start the meeting late enough so that she would have a chance to plant that tote bag in its usual place in her cubicle. We also scheduled the meeting to end by mid-morning to avoid a break-up around lunchtime. That avoided creating a situation in which Ana might feel compelled to take her tote bag to the meeting so that she could then hurry to the cafeteria for lunch. Instead, she should expect to have plenty of time to return to work in her cubicle before lunch.

Dave would have to keep Ana inside the conference room for at least an hour and a half by force of personality alone. I knew he would do so. The fact is, Dave is a very feisty guy, with a bit of a temper. When Dave summons his subordinates to a meeting, it is understood that everyone stays until Dave is satisfied that all issues have been sufficiently aired. No one walks casually out of a meeting hosted by the boss.

Still, we took no chances. We planted another asset inside the meeting— John Kavanagh, one of the counterintelligence analysts and Cuban specialists who supported me throughout the investigation. John's instructions were simple. In the unlikely event that Ana Montes should leave the room for any reason before ten-thirty (for example, should she become sick and head for the bathroom to vomit), John would reach for the telephone and call our DIAC command post to sound the alarm through a code phrase. We would have only seconds, literally, to react.

And so, at precisely 9:00 AM on Thursday morning, August 16, Dave Curtin called me on our phone in the DIAC command post and spoke a code phrase to indicate that Ana had arrived in the conference room for the meeting. I told Dave to keep her there and we would do the rest. We then dispatched Josh Mosley, the Navy technician, to Ana's general work area. Josh had supported us throughout the investigation, and he impressed me by his maturity and poise. He was very low key and unflappable under pressure, and he kept his mouth shut. My kind of guy.

Josh's job was essentially to provide a cover for action. He would distract Ana's co-workers by pretending to search for a computer glitch in the general area. It was a perfect cover story. DIA is a computer-heavy, computer-dependent agency. Computers are everywhere, and they are forever breaking down. Ana, in fact, had had a number of computer and computer-related problems during the previous six months.

DIA employees are quite used to seeing computer guys pulling up the carpeting and flooring to search for broken wires and the like. That meant that Josh was a familiar, friendly face. I knew Ana's co-workers would immediately accept him into their midst and ignore him. He could wander freely among them. It was just Josh, after all, and computer problems were rampant.

Not long after Josh arrived in the general area of Ana's co-workers, Lieutenant Schweitzer, the daytime shift supervisor for the DIA police force, initiated a telephone call to clear Montes' cubicle mate, Steve Smith, from his desk. Steve—or at least something belonging to him—was about to have an accident.

I had scouted the parking lots around the DIAC for several days before the operation, and I usually found Steve's van parked in close proximity to Ana's vehicle in the parking lot across the street. Schweitzer called Steve to tell him that his van had apparently been hit by a hit-and-run driver in the parking lot. He assured Steve that an officer had found no visible damage. But he asked Steve to join him in the DIAC lobby anyway; the two of them would walk outside to take a look. It was the oldest trick in the book, but it worked.

Carl Schweitzer was a retired cop, a former D.C. Metropolitan Police sergeant. For many years, he had worked the night shift in the Southeast section of Washington—an area that includes some of the most dangerous parts of the District of Columbia. He was a grizzled old veteran and a talker with a real talent for BS. I trusted him to keep Steve happily engaged for at least an hour.

The final component of the plan was the most risky. It involved the actual seizure of Ana's tote bag and its removal to our room for a thorough search. We had selected a "bagman" to perform that assignment. This was the crucial phase of the plan. The entire investigation could go down the tubes if Ana returned to her cubicle before her tote bag did. In fact, the operation would turn into a fiasco. Ana might engage the thief in a shouting match in her workspace, and God only knows what might happen next. It wouldn't be pretty.

I had the easiest job of all. I stayed behind in our staging area and choreographed the operation.

With Ana and Steve out of the way and their co-workers effectively distracted by Josh, the computer guy, our bagman walked down the long corridor toward Ana's cubicle. He was dressed casually, and our scenario called for him to join Josh near Ana's cubicle. The bagman had a cell phone with him. In the event that Ana left the meeting upstairs for some reason, the DIAC command post would alert the bagman via cell phone. His instructions were simple: If the phone rings, don't take the time to answer it. Just drop the tote bag where you found it, and head north out of the area. With luck, our bagman would clear the cubicle space before Ana arrived, right on his heels.

Josh and the bagman rooted around the area briefly in search of their illusory computer problem and then worked slowly into the cubicle itself. Once inside, Josh provided cover by continuing his search for the source of the computer problem. The bagman moved toward Ana's tote bag.

First, he crushed the outside of the bag with his hands to determine whether it might have disks or other items hidden within its seams. Finding that the bag was soft all around, he opened it and removed Ana's address book and a small black purse festooned with cowboy fringes. He placed them into a small toolbox provided to him earlier by Josh Mosley. Then the bagman opened the file cabinet in which Ana habitually stored her pocketbook; he placed the pocketbook into the toolbox as well, and left the area.

Josh remained behind in Ana's cubicle and continued to perform his ruse for the benefit of any co-workers who might glance his way, while the bagman marched straight down the long corridor to our DIAC command post. It must have been excruciating for him. His route back to the command post was the same path that Ana would have to take back to her cubicle. His worst nightmare, at that point, would have been the vision of Ana walking down the corridor toward him. It was a very narrow corridor, and the two of them would have brushed shoulders as they passed.

Fortunately, that didn't happen. Back in the command post, our bagman conducted a legal search of the purse and pocketbook (remember, we were operating with the FISA court's permission). He and I then walked to a nearby room to photocopy Ana's address book. The entrance to the room faced the corridor that the bagman had just passed, so we were again at some risk of discovery. I stood near the doorway to provide interference in case anyone else tried to enter the room to make copies.

We got lucky. The pocketbook contained some evidence: the prepaid phone card that Ana had used to place all of her operational calls from public telephones to Cuban pagers in New York City. Next to that card was a slip of paper. Notations on the slip matched the codes that Ana had punched into the phones to send to the pagers. This was good stuff—physical evidence that directly tied Ana Montes to telephone calls placed to the Cubans, combined with part of her communications plan for those pagers. The operation was a success.

Within thirty minutes, the search was complete and Ana's property was back in her cubicle. Neither Ana nor any of her co-workers had an inkling that anything unusual had occurred in their area that day.

We didn't find all the crypto materials we'd hoped for, but we had scored a victory of sorts with the evidence that was recovered. We also boosted Admiral Wilson's confidence that we were capable of retrieving evidence under difficult circumstances. The operation bought us a little more time for the FBI to continue its investigation.

The next day, Friday, August 17, Ana and Bill left the Washington area en route to Cape Cod, where they participated in Bill's family reunion. They would remain out of the area until the following Wednesday, August 22.

16

SEPTEMBER 11

THE TWO WEEKS AFTER OUR SEARCH of Ana's tote bag were uneventful. Pressure continued to build to lift the freeze on external analyst assignments, and given the seemingly poor prospects for fresh developments in the investigation, Admiral Wilson was inclined to bring the matter to a close. On September 10, he proposed a meeting comprised only of Defense Department members to develop a departmental position on the future of the investigation. The admiral would host the meeting, representatives of the Office of the Secretary of Defense would participate, and a position would be formed and subsequently presented to the FBI and the Justice Department. At least, that was the proposed scenario.

The principal players checked their schedules and agreed to meet on September 21 for their discussion. On September 11, 2001, however, the planned meeting was overcome by events. The terrorist attacks on the World Trade Center towers in Manhattan, followed by a similar attack on the Pentagon and the crash of a commercial jetliner in Pennsylvania, changed everyone's priorities.

I witnessed part of the Pentagon attack that day from a colleague's office on the seventh floor of the DIA's Arlington office building. His office in the northeast corner of the building offers a panoramic view of Washington, D.C. In the distance, the Washington Monument pierces the sky, and beyond it is the dome of the U.S. Capitol.

The Pentagon can't actually be seen from the office. It is hidden by the trees that dot the hillsides of Arlington National Cemetery to the east. But we know its general location beneath us. I drive past the Pentagon every day while commuting to and from work. Ronald Reagan Washington National Airport is also largely hidden from view, just to the south of the Pentagon. We can't see its terminal buildings, but the path that aircraft take on approach to National Airport runs right past our windows. We watch them go past every day. We don't see the planes that fly from another major Washington airport, Dulles, more than half an hour to the west on the other side of our building.

For me, the first news of the attacks came when I walked past my colleague's office that morning and observed several of my co-workers huddled inside watching the news on a wall-mounted television. An aircraft had hit one of the World Trade Center towers and speculation was already rife among those gathered in the office that the crash was the result of a terrorist attack, not a freak accident. As we watched the news, another aircraft hit the second tower, confirming our suspicion. This was no accident.

Like Americans everywhere that day, we remained glued to the television for quite a while. Thoughts of an attack on Washington were given voice, and several of us nervously scanned the skies for indications that an aircraft was headed our way. After nearly an hour, the others drifted back to their desks to speak in hushed tones about the attack, leaving me alone in the office, still watching the television.

I was the first to notice the puff of smoke that appeared over the ridgeline just beyond the trees to our east. My first thought was that a house might have caught fire. But then I recalled that there was no housing in that area, only Arlington Cemetery. Beyond that was the George Washington Parkway, and beyond that, the Pentagon.

That first puff of smoke turned into an expanding billow, changing in color from white to gray. It occurred to me that there might have been a major accident on the parkway beyond my view and I alerted the others in my office to the smoke, which by then dominated a good portion of the view to the east. Minutes later, a network correspondent announced that the Pentagon had been hit by an aircraft. We were stunned.

I didn't see the aircraft strike the Pentagon, despite the fact that I was looking toward the window at the time of the attack. We learned later that the aircraft that struck the Pentagon had taken off from Dulles Airport, about twenty-five miles to our rear as we looked out over the Potomac.

One member of our staff reported later that she observed a commercial aircraft circling the center of Washington minutes prior to the attack—a flight pattern that was prohibited by law and likely caught her eye owing to its unusual path. But the aircraft apparently circled back to the west and beyond our view. I never saw it. In its final glide toward the Pentagon, the aircraft flew from the southwest, which would have been just beyond my field of vision.

I spent the rest of the day expecting another strike on Washington. The White House and the Capitol had not been hit—both were obvious high-value targets—and the Pentagon had been struck only once, so I fully expected another strike at any moment. It was too early for anger, and fear never entered the picture. I simply recall an overwhelming sense that there was more to come that day. As we later learned, of course, another strike was intended. But thanks to the actions of its passengers, the fourth hijacked plane crashed in Pennsylvania instead of reaching its target in Washington.

Seven DIA employees died in the attack on the Pentagon, including a close professional acquaintance of my wife, and many other DIA employees were injured. Admiral Wilson and his staff were spared but had to work out of other offices in the Pentagon for several days while the smoke and other noxious gases vented from their section of the building.

Ana's boyfriend Bill was in town that day. With all U.S. airports shut down in the wake of the attack, Bill was stuck. He couldn't return to Miami, so he stayed with Ana.

A few days later, President Bush declared war on the terrorists and the nations that harbored them. With that pronouncement, I knew that the Ana Montes investigation was nearing an end, and soon. Admiral Wilson and the secretary of defense would never allow Ana to continue her employment at the Department of Defense while the country was at war. I called Steve McCoy at the FBI, who agreed with that assessment. We had only to determine when and how the end game of the investigation would be played.

The DoD kicked into a war footing, and that included DIA. Routine work was set aside, and our analysts organized themselves to process the war plan that was sure to come out of the operations (J3) staff in the Pentagon. Intelligence and operations always work side by side during times of war to ensure that American warfighters receive the best information available about their adversaries. DIA employees stationed in the Pentagon and across the river in the DIAC buzzed with activity.

Those assigned to the Pentagon returned to work the day after the September 11 attack and continued to work endless hours for days on end thereafter, despite the threat and fear of additional attacks that could have been launched against the building. Each one deserves our praise and respect. As they came to work, they understood the danger they faced. Many were also still mourning friends and colleagues wounded or killed in the attack.

The southwest corner of the Pentagon was a blackened shell that continued to burn for days after the attack. The roof caught fire, and smoke and gas poured through the building. Although another strike could come at any time, those brave men and women remained at their posts, carrying out the order that their commander in chief had issued to plan the opening phase of the war against terrorism, the war in Afghanistan. We now know that, under the most stressful circumstances imaginable, they planned it well.

By Friday, September 14, Ana Montes was also fully engaged in planning DIA's support to the war effort. Her branch chief officially transferred that date to his next Army assignment, and Ana assumed the duties of branch chief and acting division chief. Dave Curtin let us know that, owing to Ana's seniority and experience, she had been selected to serve as one of several analytical team leaders whose teams would process target information from the operations staff in the Pentagon.

The targets had not yet been selected. It was understood that Afghanistan was on our scope, but the J3 operations people in the Pentagon were still working to develop their target lists. Once they made their selections, analysts at DIA and the U.S. Central Command in Tampa, Florida, would review those lists and update them as necessary.

By that Friday, Ana was involved in planning how to organize and train our analysts to process imagery and other source information in support of the warfighters. But she didn't have her hands on the war plans yet. Meanwhile, Bill managed to get out of town to return to his duties in Miami.

During the week, there had been talk among the DIA analysts about possible targets for the war on terrorism. That Afghanistan would be attacked was a foregone conclusion. Still, Cuba remained on the State Department's list of countries that supported international terrorism, and some thought that the United States might finally settle the Cuban issue by force. Ana simply had to reach out to Havana.

After work on Friday, Ana drove home and then set out on foot toward the National Zoo, just a few blocks away. She entered the zoo by the pedestrian gate and walked for some distance inside before retracing her steps back to the entrance. By coming back the same way, she'd completed a standard surveillance detection route while inside the zoo. It was obvious that she intended to engage in some kind of operational activity.

At the entrance to the zoo, she approached a public telephone and placed two back-to-back telephone calls to a pager in New York City. She must have had a lot to say, because the pager could not accept in one call all of the numeric codes that Ana wished to transmit.

Admiral Wilson had been very busy after September 11, but Ana Montes was never far from his mind. On Monday, September 17, Wilson discussed the situation with Drew Winneberger and announced his decision. Ana would never place her hands on the war plans or any information related to them. Period. He wanted her out of the agency immediately.

By this time, we were frantically scrambling to put additional coverage in place against Ana. We thought she might be prepared to pass defense information to the Cubans—an act that could lead to a charge of treason during a time of war if the evidence demonstrated that Ana knew or should have known the Cubans would pass her information along to the Taliban in Afghanistan. Drew pleaded for additional time on behalf of the FBI. Admiral Wilson offered only to think about it and scheduled a meeting for the next afternoon to discuss the situation. He was in no mood to take additional risks.

On Tuesday, September 18, we essentially abandoned hope of catching Ana in the act of passing defense information to the Cubans. The writing was on the wall, and everyone accepted it without further discussion: No one was willing to risk the loss of war planning information to the Cubans or to anyone else. The FBI shifted gears and began to prepare for their final move, the arrest of Ana Montes for conspiracy to commit espionage.

That afternoon, Admiral Wilson learned during our meeting in his office that Ana and some other analysts were to participate in some training on target processing the next weekend, September 22 and 23. Ana might gain some initial access to targeting information, however, on Friday. The admiral's decision was clear. His drop-dead date and time for removing Ana Montes from the agency was Friday morning. He wanted her out of the agency as early that morning as possible.

Steve and his team were very busy people that week. Steve was fully engaged in the process of drafting the affidavit that would support an arrest warrant for Ana Montes. That draft would make its way through many layers of review, both within the FBI and the Department of Justice, before Steve could swear to its contents before a federal judge in time for the arrest on Friday.

Pete, Steve's co-case agent, organized the FBI teams that would effect Ana's arrest and the searches of her workspace in the DIAC, her vehicle, her safe-deposit box, and her residence. Nothing was left to chance. The FBI always plans every phase of every case. Like Boy Scouts, they are always prepared, and every member of every team understood his or her role.

A decision was made to arrest Ana Montes at work in the DIAC. Though the odds of obtaining her cooperation during an interview were slim at best, they would improve if the FBI attempted an interview prior to placing her under arrest. The best place and time for that conversation was in the DIAC on Friday morning. We wanted it to be done in a low-profile, low-key manner. No theatrics.

In my role as Steve's action officer in the DIAC, I assumed responsibility for the logistics of the interview, the arrest, the search of Ana's cubicle following the arrest, and follow-on actions that were related to her arrest. Steve and Pete would conduct the interview and finally place Ana under arrest. I was simply a stage director, operating behind the scenes to ensure that everything ran smoothly.

On Wednesday, I drove downtown to the Washington field office to meet with Steve, Pete, and some of their team leaders. I observed Steve in conversation with an attorney outside the FBI building, and I waited until they broke before approaching Steve. Steve was obviously under a lot of stress, but he was handling it well. There was a lot to be done, and he was responsible for everything.

Steve and I took a minute to walk and talk outside in the sunshine, and I remember talking philosophically with him about the sudden end of the case, and cracking a few jokes to ease the weight of stress that had accumulated during the past few days. Steve and I had been working closely together on the Ana Montes case for about a year. It had been a long and tough road, and in some ways we regretted that it was coming to an end. I'm really glad that in the midst of all the activity that occurred during the final days of the Montes investigation, in the midst of the many telephone calls and meetings and decisions and the many actions that each of us was to take in the days ahead, Steve and I managed to steal some time away from the madness just to talk together in the sunshine for a while. For me, those were the most pleasant moments of the entire case.

Thursday, September 20, the day before Ana Montes' arrest, was an extraordinarily busy day for me. I wrote an operations plan to cover the logistics of the arrest, Ana's removal from the DIAC, the search of her cubicle, and perhaps the most important action of the day—breaking the news of Ana's arrest to her co-workers.

The latter action was foremost in my mind. We were at war, and Ana's co-workers were about to commence the processing of target packages for the war in Afghanistan. If ever they needed a sense of serenity and focus in their professional lives, this was it. Yet the arrest of Ana Montes—someone with whom many of them had worked for about a decade—would naturally upset and distract even the strongest among them. We had to help them deal with the trauma of Ana's arrest. So the timing and the framing of the announcement of the arrest was important to us.

At the end of the day, I called Steve at his office to assure him that I'd considered every detail. I launched into my briefing almost immediately, but Steve stopped me short with, "Scott, Scott. Listen. Do I really need to hear all the details?" He was as close to exasperation as I'd ever heard him. It dawned on me that Steve was up to his ears just then, preparing for the interview of Ana Montes—one of the most important interviews of his professional life. The last thing he needed at that moment was a distraction from me or from anyone else. "No," I acknowledged. "You're right. You only need to know that I've taken care of everything over here and that it'll go smoothly tomorrow." We were ready.

17

END GAME

THE BULK OF DIA'S SECURITY OFFICES are located in the agency's office building in Arlington, Virginia, the same building from which I had seen smoke coming from the Pentagon on September 11. We have limited space in the DIAC itself. I arranged for the use of space within the offices of the inspector general, on the fourth floor of the DIAC, for the interview and the arrest of Ana Montes.

The inspector general has a large suite of offices at the northeast corner of the DIAC. Individual offices line the north wall of the suite, with views of the U.S. Capitol and the Washington Monument. Bud Uthe, the inspector general, offered his conference room for Ana's interview. He would be out of town on business on Friday, but his assistant inspector general for administration, Leroy Elfmann, would lend a hand as needed.

My wife worked for Bud Uthe as an assistant inspector general for inspections, but she was in training at the time. I commandeered her office to serve as the FBI's command post on the scene. Drew Winneberger would also be on the scene at the time of Ana's arrest, so I borrowed Bobby Speegle's office, during his temporary absence from work, to serve as Drew's command post.

Although Ana had no history of heart ailments or other serious medical disorders, we also had a nurse on standby. Dave Curtin had told us Ana had collapsed several years earlier upon learning that she had been unexpectedly promoted. We prepared for the worst, placing the nurse in a room near the conference room. The nurse had a wheelchair handy, as well as everything that might be required in the event Ana suffered anything from a fainting spell to a heart attack.

Thus a cast of thousands seemed to be on hand to spring the surprise on Ana Montes that she was under arrest by the FBI for conspiracy to commit espionage. Leroy Elfmann, though, was the only member of the inspector general's office present that day who knew exactly what was about to occur. The word given to everyone else was simply that security was interviewing someone in the conference room that morning, and the inspector general's staff should ignore us.

By ten o'clock, everyone was set. Steve and Pete were safely tucked away inside the conference room. One of my colleagues and the registered nurse were closeted nearby. Molly, an FBI special agent, was also a member of the arrest team; she staffed the FBI command post. Drew Winneberger sat patiently inside Bobby Speegle's office.

I had arranged a pretext telephone call to bring Ana downstairs to the inspector general's office area. To handle that detail, I called once again upon Dave Curtin. Dave had been running around DIA for days with his hair on fire, beating the war drums and preparing his large staff of analysts to handle the surge of requirements that were certain to flow from the Pentagon during the coming months. He was really a very busy guy. But he understood the need for his participation in this final exercise. Ana would listen to him, and she would obey a direct request by Dave to meet him in the inspector general's conference room.

Dave placed his call from the FBI command post at about 10:15 AM. He was sharp. He began his conversation with Ana by recounting some crisis that had arisen that very morning, just one in a myriad of such matters with which Dave had had to deal during the past week or so. Ana was aware of the current crisis, and she commiserated with Dave. After a minute of such conversation, Dave switched gears. "In the middle of all this, Ana, I get summoned down to the IG office to deal with an issue on one of your subordinates. And frankly, I don't have time for it."

Dave knew that Ana was serving, temporarily, as an acting division chief. Whatever issue the inspector general might be addressing about one of her subordinates was of concern to Ana. "I need you to come down here to deal with this for me," he said. "And then I've got to get back upstairs for a meeting with Caryne," referring to Caryne Wagner. "I'm down here with Leroy Elfmann. Just come on down, and Mr. Elfmann can explain this thing to you."

That was Dave's last action in support of the Ana Montes investigation. He'd been my go-to guy since the day that we first briefed him into the case. I believe he performed admirably. Dave did not go upstairs to participate in a meeting with Caryne Wagner after completing his call to Ana Montes. He joined Drew Winneberger in Bobby Speegle's office to witness the very end of the case.

After Dave's call, Leroy Elfmann told his receptionist to expect a visit by an employee named Ana Montes. She should simply direct Ana toward Leroy's office, at the end of the hall. I slipped into my wife's office and waited there with Molly.

A couple of minutes later Ana arrived and Leroy ushered her into the conference room, where Steve and Pete were already waiting. We passed the word along to the Washington field office, where Steve's supervisor and others had their own command post.

There was no way to know just how long Steve, Pete, and Ana might remain in the conference room. The longer, the better. Steve hoped to plant a few thoughts in Ana's brain from the outset, I was sure, just to get and hold her attention. With luck, Ana would listen as they advised her of her Miranda rights, and then continue to listen until she was persuaded to cooperate.

No such luck. Steve had his say, and he advised her of her rights. But Ana invoked her right to silence and her right to consult with legal counsel. That ended the interview process on the spot. Steve informed Ana that she was under arrest, and the door to the conference room opened some twenty minutes after Ana first entered the room. Molly searched Ana after her arrest.

I had arranged for Gator and Bo Edmundson, a lieutenant from our DIA police force, to escort the arrest team out of the building. Bo waited at the end of the hall. As the arrest team approached, I briefly held them in place until Bo could secure one of the service elevators for the ride down to the basement level of the building.

The arrest team consisted of Steve, Pete, and Molly. I asked Steve to ensure that he seized Ana's DIA badge before leaving the building. The U.S. Marshals would presumably have seized the badge during their in-processing of Ana as a prisoner, but I wanted Steve, as the FBI's senior case agent on the investigation, to have that badge as a remembrance of our joint effort on the case.

Ana never looked my way. Or if she did, I didn't catch her in the act. I did glance at her, though, and I found her to be as cool as ice. There was no sign of emotion on her face. Except for the handcuffs on her wrists, she might have been standing in line to purchase a ticket at the movies for all the emotion she displayed. It was eerie.

And then they were gone. That was the last I saw of Ana Montes. I had too much work to do just then to reflect upon that moment. But I recall it now as surreal. I'm glad that I refrained from saying anything to her. At that point, there was really nothing to say.

Bo sealed the elevator and escorted the arrest team down to the basement level. From there, it was a fairly short walk down a corridor to the DIAC service entrance where the FBI had parked their cars that morning. Gator and Bo led the arrest team down the corridor. They passed a number of DIA employees as they walked along, but no one noticed anything out of the ordinary. There was no commotion. Ana Montes very quietly left the building, never to return.

18

THE AFTERMATH

AS SOON AS THE ARREST TEAM ENTERED the elevator to take Ana Montes downstairs, I hustled our nurse and her security escort to an adjacent elevator to follow. We were taking no chances with Ana's health while she remained on the premises. If she fainted or suffered any other medical malady while the team escorted her from the DIAC, our nurse would be prepared to assist. Fortunately, the team left without incident.

With Ana's arrest out of the way, we popped the bubble of ignorance that had surrounded her for nearly a year. Two actions were launched simultaneously: briefing her co-workers and beginning a meticulous search of her cubicle for anything that might be of evidentiary value.

Drew Winneberger and Dave Curtin walked to Ana's work area, assembled her mystified co-workers, and marched them upstairs to a conference room for the briefing. An FBI evidence collection team swept in immediately after her co-workers left and cordoned off Ana's cubicle with police tape. It was a very smooth operation.

Upstairs, Drew addressed Ana's co-workers. Both he and Admiral Wilson were sensitive to the need to deal properly with the emotional trauma that was bound to result from Drew's announcement, so a team of counselors from DIA's Employee Assistance Program stood by in the wings to assist. After a brief personal introduction, Drew got directly to the point.

"I have an announcement to make concerning RAL-1 employee Ana Montes," he began. RAL-1 was the internal office designator for Ana's office within DIA. "Ana Montes was arrested by the FBI a short while ago. The FBI arrested Ana under suspicion that she engaged in a conspiracy to commit espionage against the United States. There will likely be a short public announcement about the arrest later tonight, or possibly this weekend. The director will issue a statement to DIA employees sometime next week. Ana will not return to work."

I'd drafted Drew's announcement. I wanted him to say the word "arrest" several times during the briefing to ensure that it had a chance to sink in. The human brain can process only so much information, especially when the information is delivered verbally. Repetition of the word "arrest" would ensure that particular fact would sink in, even if the rest of his message fell by the wayside. I added the statement "Ana will not return to work" to emphasize that this was not a mistake, that her co-workers had not misunderstood the announcement, and that the action was final, not a temporary bump in the road after which Ana might be expected to return to work.

"I know that this is a shock," Drew continued, "and that you have a lot of questions. We cannot answer your questions at this time. That fact is bound to cause frustration for you—we know that. But we ask for your patience. The entire story concerning Ana's arrest by the FBI will come out eventually. In the meantime, we simply have to allow the legal process to work."

Drew then addressed their emotions and how to deal with them. "You are going to experience a wide range of emotions over the next few days and weeks. This is a shock. You are going to feel confused, frustrated, angry, and sad. You will experience denial and disbelief. Those are normal human emotions, and you are going to experience them. But you can't keep them bottled up inside. You have to vent those emotions. So talk to someone about how the arrest of Ana Montes makes you feel. Find someone in whom you can confide your feelings and then do so. We encourage you to meet with Employee Assistance counselors to work through the difficult days ahead."

Drew then provided some guidance for the immediate future. "You will naturally talk to one another about Ana's arrest during the days ahead. You have to do so, in order to vent your emotions. But we do have some Do's and Don't's for you, and we ask you to follow these simple rules." By this point in Drew's presentation, I expected Ana's co-workers to have processed no more than "Oh, my gosh, Ana really has been arrested!" Their brains would be addled and overloaded, and we couldn't realistically expect them to comprehend and remember instructions for the future. But we provided some direction anyway, in hopes that at least a handful would actually take in the entire message and later guide their colleagues along our recommended paths of behavior. Shock and disbelief were registered on every face in the conference room.

"Do not initiate telephone calls to anyone outside of RAL," Drew continued. "That means: Don't call your usual contacts at Southcom, J2, CIA, NIMA [National Imagery and Mapping Agency], NSA, the State Department, or other agencies. They will hear of Ana's arrest soon enough. Keep your discussions about Ana to yourselves. Consider Ana's arrest to be an in-house matter, and act accordingly."

We hoped to minimize speculative gossip about Ana's situation for a couple of reasons. The first was Operation Enduring Freedom, the intensive effort in the wake of the September 11 attacks to remove the Taliban from power in Afghanistan and to attack al-Qaeda bases there. Ana's former co-workers and analysts throughout the U.S. intelligence community would begin supporting the operation in earnest the very next day, a Saturday. This was no time to lose focus. We wanted to minimize the distraction from that mission that Ana's situation was bound to cause throughout the intelligence community.

We also wanted to prevent our analysts from exchanging information about Ana with those who might someday be called upon to testify regarding Ana's case. People should testify in court to what they know, not what they hear from others. An exchange of speculative gossip about Ana could taint later testimony in court, and we hoped to minimize the complications that might arise from gossip.

Drew continued his instructions, turning now to the subject of incoming calls about Ana. "You can expect lots of calls from your usual contacts during the next few workdays," he said. "People are curious, and they will call. When people call, you should tell them, 'I'm sorry. I wish I could talk to you about that. But I have been instructed to not discuss Ana Montes at all. We will have to talk about something else.'" We wanted Ana's co-workers to discuss their feelings with one another, but we did not want them to speculate about the basis for Ana's arrest. That was asking a bit much, we knew, but we had to make the effort.

Next, Drew put Ana's co-workers on notice that the FBI would be interviewing some, if not all, of them in the coming days and weeks. "You are the people who worked closest to Ana Montes. You are her co-workers. So the

FBI naturally has an interest in speaking with each of you." The interviews, he explained, would probably happen right here, in the DIAC building.

I had already prepared a list of Ana's co-workers and colleagues for the FBI to interview, summarizing each one's known relationship with Ana and the issues to which that person might be able to speak with authority. In general, Drew said, those present should wait to hear from the FBI. Anyone with information about Ana Montes and espionage that the FBI should know "sooner rather than later" was told to contact me. No one called me to request an immediate interview.

We also had to prepare Ana's co-workers for the sight of FBI agents at work in her cubicle. More than one agent was involved in the search effort, and the agents had parked a couple of flatbed dollies nearby to haul Ana's materials away. It was a bit of a spectacle. Drew told the group that the search was already underway; FBI personnel were in the cubicle and would be for several hours. "For the time being," he explained, "we cannot allow you to return to your own cubicles. You will be permitted to return to your own cubicles sometime after the FBI has completed its work in Ana's cubicle." Several people were subsequently given a chance to retrieve their purses and wallets, but they were not allowed to remain for long.

Finally, Drew stated clearly, "The arrest of Ana Montes was in no way connected to the terrorist attacks against the United States that occurred last week." Of course, the *timing* of Ana's arrest was related to the attacks. With wartime conditions suddenly upon us, we could no longer let Ana remain active as a spy. What this statement meant was that there was no connection between the September 11 attacks and the Ana Montes espionage case.

After the briefing, most of Ana's co-workers, barred from their usual work space, went down to the cafeteria to pass the time and exchange commiserations. Their initial reaction to the news was predictable and universal: shock and disbelief. More than one person broke down in tears, and one began sobbing uncontrollably. Several accepted the assistance offered by professional counselors.

The rest of my day was spent tying up administrative loose ends. I kept busy, as did Gator. For Pete and Steve McCoy, the hard part of the investigation had just begun. As my own role was winding down, theirs was shifting from one high gear to another as they dealt with daily demands from the Department of Justice for information to support the prosecution of Ana Montes. I played no role in that effort.

Later that day, I wandered up to Ana's cubicle to check on the status of the FBI's search effort. Marty Scheina, Ana's second-level supervisor, saw me in the area and waved me into his office. He just needed to talk—to vent.

When he hired Ana Montes at DIA, nearly sixteen years earlier, Marty had considered her an ideal, if possibly overqualified, candidate for the vacant intelligence research specialist billet he was trying to fill. He was immensely pleased at securing Ana for that position. Over the years, Marty had continued to supervise Ana, right up until the day of her arrest. He'd watched her develop into one of the finest analysts in the agency, indeed, one of the finest analysts in the intelligence community. He had supported her as faithfully as a well-served supervisor can possibly support a stellar employee. And now this.

Marty was the very embodiment of dismay. He was completely at a loss to comprehend what had just happened. At that moment, Marty just needed someone to listen and to tell him that he had done nothing wrong himself. He could not fathom Ana's actions. He had spent more than twenty years in the intelligence business, virtually all of that time as a Latin America specialist. Ana Montes had negated much of what he had accomplished. He felt that his entire professional career had been for nothing. I could not argue against that assessment, but it wasn't his fault. He'd have to start over. The sense of betrayal for Marty was both deeply personal and professional.

I later spent some time with Ana's cubicle mate Steve. Steve told me that he accepted the announcement of Ana's arrest the moment the words were spoken. He did not experience a moment of disbelief, though he'd never imagined that Ana might be engaged in espionage or any other unlawful activity. He simply accepted it as fact. And then he got angry. Steve had probably been closer to Ana, on a personal level, than anyone else at DIA. He had shared a cubicle with her for about five years, and during that time they had developed a personal rapport, if not a true friendship. Like Marty, Steve felt a deep sense of personal betrayal, and he could not forgive her.

I could go on, but I'll describe just one more person's reaction. Lourdes Talbot was the youngest analyst in Ana's division, a Princeton graduate who was exceptionally bright and warmly personal. Like Ana, she was of Puerto Rican descent. Ana had taken Lourdes under her professional wing. For Lourdes, Ana had been a role model—a strong, independent, smart, and capable analyst, seemingly devoted to her trade, who exhibited a work ethic matched by none. Lourdes, too, took Ana's actions as a betrayal of trust. Tears welled easily at the corners of her eyes when she spoke about her experiences with Ana at DIA.

None of Ana's immediate co-workers, the people she worked with every day, had ever suspected that she was a spy. She had fooled them all. None of them communicated with Ana again.

A few of Ana's colleagues, both at DIA and at other agencies within the community, later claimed that they "just knew" that Ana was a spy or that her arrest had not surprised them all that much. But none of them, except Reg Brown, had stepped forward to make their views known to security officials before Ana's arrest. I suspect that their views of Ana had the advantage of 20/20 hindsight.

My active role in the Ana Montes investigation ended shortly after Ana's arrest. I was, quite honestly, tired of dealing with her by then and happy to have reached the end. I still had to deal with an occasional question or request from Steve or Pete, but I walked as far away from the case as possible after Ana left the DIAC for the last time.

Neither Gator nor I attended the small number of formal hearings at the federal courthouse in Washington, D.C., on the Montes case. We both felt the same way. Satisfaction was not to be found in the spectacle of her misery but only in the knowledge that we'd done our best to neutralize her efforts inside our agency.

Ana retained Plato Cacheris as her legal counsel—a good choice. His experience in dealing with national security matters, specifically espionage, was unmatched by any other member of his profession. His previous clients included convicted CIA spy Aldrich Ames and convicted FBI spy Robert Hanssen.

Cacheris and the Department of Justice reached a plea agreement, which Ana signed. Its terms required her to plead guilty to one count of conspiracy to commit espionage, to submit to a debriefing by the FBI, and to serve a twenty-five-year sentence. During the debriefing, Ana was expected to fully disclose her activities on behalf of the Cuban Intelligence Service. Her truthfulness would be tested by FBI polygraph examiners, and the deal depended on it. Because she had agreed to plead guilty, there would be no trial—only a sentencing hearing after much of the debriefing was complete.

Ana was sentenced to twenty-five years on October 16, 2002, more than a year after her arrest. At the sentencing, she read a statement that sought, among other things, to explain, if not justify, her espionage. She stated in part, "Your honor, I engaged in the activity that brought me before you because I obeyed my conscience rather than the law. I believe our government's policy towards Cuba is cruel and unfair, profoundly unneighborly, and I felt morally obligated to help the island defend itself from our efforts to impose our values and our political system on it. . . . I did what I thought right to counter a grave injustice."

She had kept busy doing so. Based on the information gathered before and after her arrest, we now know that Ana spied for the Cubans for nearly sixteen years. For much of that time, the Cubans would broadcast coded messages to Ana several times a week. After receiving the messages on her shortwave radio, she decrypted them using a system provided to her by Cuban intelligence. As we had surmised, Ana didn't remove materials from work to pass along to her Cuban handlers—the information was in her head. Upon arrival at home each afternoon, Ana stored her recollections of the day's events on a floppy disk.

For years, she handed disks to her Cuban handlers about twice a month during meetings in the Washington area. At the meetings, Ana also provided verbal briefings to the Cubans and answered their debriefing questions. Communication via pagers was simply an alternate system at that time.

Ana's long-standing routine was interrupted by the arrests in September 1998 of the Wasp network in Miami, Florida. The personal meetings in Washington ended shortly thereafter, a fact that accounted for our failure to catch her red-handed in a meeting.

The government of Cuba, at least, seemed to appreciate her efforts. A few months after Ana's arrest, Foreign Minister Felipe Perez Roque commented in an online exchange, "I feel deep respect and admiration for Ana Belen Montes. She has already spoken for herself about her relationship with Cuba and her motivations." He noted that she had claimed to have received no money from Cuba and added, "I can confirm that. She acted compelled by ethics and an admirable sense of justice." He closed with the thought, "The day aggression and terrorist attacks against Cuba stop and we are allowed to live in peace it will no longer be necessary for men and women of the moral stature of Ana Belen Montes . . . to sacrifice their lives, their families, and personal interests to defend our people's tranquility and right to live."

I can understand the foreign minister's sentiments. But I align my own more closely with those expressed by U.S. District Court Judge Ricardo Urbina. As he stated at Ana's sentencing, "If you can't love your country, then at the very least you should do it no wrong."

19

NO ORDINARY SPY

ANA MONTES WAS NOT SIMPLY A SPY. She was a super spy on the order of Aldrich Ames at the CIA; the FBI's Robert Hanssen; John Walker, whose spy ring betrayed the U.S. Navy's top-secret codes to the KGB; the U.S. Army's Clyde Lee Conrad, who gave the U.S. and NATO war plans for Europe to Hungary, which passed them to the Soviets; and Jonathan Pollard, the naval intelligence analyst who spied for Israel.

Some have speculated that a wily Cuban intelligence officer spotted Ana Montes and tricked or verbally seduced her into her role as a spy, as though Ana were some kind of naive victim. But that is not the case. Ana was not a foolish innocent who helplessly fell into someone's trap. She did not enter into the business of espionage without realizing what she was doing. Once she began spying, she was truly a master spy. She was serious about her espionage from day one. She spied from within DIA for almost sixteen years, from September 30, 1985, until the day of her arrest on September 21, 2001, making her one of the longest-running spies in U.S. history. She operated alone. And she didn't accept a dime in payment for her services.

Ana Montes was a true believer. She spied out of a conviction that Fidel Castro was both the savior of the Cuban people and a champion of oppressed masses throughout the world, particularly in Latin America. Castro was her hero, and Ana served as his eyes and ears—and, in a sense, his voice—inside the

U.S. intelligence community. I doubt the Cubans ever seriously pressed her to accept money for her work. Ana would have been offended had they done so.

Far from tiring of her endeavors over the years, moreover, she celebrated her own success. Early in the investigation, we gathered together as much background information about Ana as we possibly could. Most of it was the kind of superficial information that could be discreetly obtained. One such item was her leave history. "Leave" is military jargon for time taken off work— vacations, sick time, and so on. It's all categorized as leave by the military. We reviewed Ana's leave history, searching for patterns. Patterns of behavior tell a lot about a person, and we wanted to learn as much as we could about Ana's life and her routine. One such pattern struck us as odd. She habitually took leave on September 30.

Now, that might not seem so strange at first glance. Employees commonly take their vacations at the same time every year, but there was, nevertheless, something peculiar about it. Some years she took leave on September 30, but *only* on September 30. If September 30 happened to fall on a Wednesday, for example, she'd take that Wednesday off work and return to work on Thursday as usual. Sometimes she'd take a vacation and other times she'd call in sick. But it was always September 30, and sometimes only September 30. That drove us batty.

We began to look for something in her life that could give that specific date significance, but we came up empty-handed. September 30 was not her birthday, nor that of any member of her immediate or extended family as far as we knew. Was it perhaps the date of a loved one's death? Not that we could discern. The wedding date for her parents, her brothers, her sister, an aunt, an uncle, a niece, a nephew, anyone in the family? No. The birthday of a best friend or acquaintance, perhaps? We checked. Nada. Was it some kind of religious holiday, anniversary, or annual celebration? Again, no. Or was it a date with some special political or historical significance? Well, nothing that appeared relevant to Ana, anyway.

We scraped and raked through what we knew of this woman's life three ways from Sunday, but we could attach no special meaning to that date. Then one day it dawned on Gator that September 30, as I mentioned near the beginning of this chapter, was the anniversary of Ana's first day on the job with DIA. September 30 was the date she was sworn in as a DIA employee, the date she was first processed into the agency.

Now, I've known many, many federal employees during my twenty-plus years of federal service. None of them were so enamored of their jobs, so delighted with their federal employment, so exceedingly happy to work for Uncle Sam that they actually took off their anniversary date to celebrate. In fact, as far as I know, I happen to be the happiest federal employee ever. I absolutely *love* my job. But I couldn't tell you my exact anniversary date to save my life. It's either in late July or early August. Take your pick. I have no idea.

So Ana's celebration of her start date at DIA was odd, but what were we to make of it? Here's an employee of astounding accomplishment on the job who has no time for her co-workers, whom she generally avoids like the plague. Are we to believe that she's celebrating the fact she has this particular job, the joy of coming to work each day in her shared DIA cubicle? I don't think so. She didn't seem to celebrate anything. It made no sense.

Then we theorized that the date had some very special significance to her life. September 30 was the date she first set foot into DIA. Could it also have been the date that she first penetrated the U.S. intelligence community at the behest of her Cuban handlers? Was it possible that she took September 30 off every year to celebrate the anniversary of her success at having become the greatest spy in the history of the Cuban Intelligence Service? Was she toasting her own success at spying? Yes, that was possible, and it made sense.

It was the only theory that made any sense at all, which dumbfounded us at that early stage of the investigation. It suggested that Ana Montes had been spying for the Cubans for approximately sixteen years, her entire career with DIA—from day one. It suggested that she had entered her employment with DIA as a spy, already fully recruited and possibly tasked by the Cubans to secure employment with a federal agency that promised access to information that was of interest to Cuba.

If so, she'd hit the jackpot when she secured employment as a DIA analyst. Remember that in 1985, Ana had also applied for positions at the Library of Congress, at the Office of Naval Intelligence, and at the Arms Control and Disarmament Agency. Instead, she landed a job with an agency that gave her intimate access to the very heart of the beast—the U.S. military. That made September 30, her first day at DIA, a date to remember.

American spies of the recent past, like Aldrich Ames and Robert Hanssen, were a danger to the United States and of value to their foreign handlers because of their access to the nation's secrets. That was, of course, more than bad enough. What makes Ana Montes so extraordinary, though, is that she not only had access to the United States' innermost secrets but also actually *created* many of the secrets—the highly classified assessments representing what we thought we knew about Cuba. In the wake of her arrest, the intelligence community has had to reassess the validity of every judgment she supported or established during the previous sixteen years. The combination of access and influence made Ana, in my humble opinion, one of the most dangerous spies in U.S. history.

The greatest real or potential damage to our national security from the secrets that she stole had little to do, directly, with Cuba. It had much to do with Cuba's friends. Like other nations, Cuba shares intelligence with countries whose interests are in line with its own interests. Information provided to Cuba by Ana Montes would have naturally found its way to nations such as Russia, China, Libya, Iran, Iraq, Syria, North Korea, and, potentially, any and every country or political movement that opposes the United States. Information is currency. Castro could spend it as he liked to advance his own interests, and his greatest interest was in keeping the United States on the defensive. He was not our friend. He almost certainly provided information derived from Ana Montes to the United States' adversaries.

Ana was able to acquire such secrets through her work as the government's top Cuba analyst, of course. But she also benefited from the information sharing that occurs every day in the intelligence community. DIA does not operate in a vacuum. For example, the CIA and DIA share responsibility, along with other members of the community, for strategic intelligence, such as the threat to the United States posed by foreign intercontinental ballistic missiles. The two agencies also overlap on international trafficking of illegal narcotics, counterterrorism, and nonproliferation of weapons of mass destruction. Specialists from DIA work with counterparts from a long list of intelligence agencies, all focused on slightly different aspects of the same overarching issue. Networking is necessary to ensure that nothing of importance falls through the cracks.

The dynamics of shared responsibilities and common missions, combined with the human desire among analysts to associate with people who share their interests, leads the analysts to share information—within limits. The CIA, NSA, and FBI, in particular, have developed reputations for being stingy with their information. They may go so far as to provide generic summaries of information to other agencies when necessary, but they do so only reluctantly, and they rarely share information that could reveal their sources or methods.

Still, even the most stringent efforts to protect proprietary information from disclosure to counterparts at the DIA, Drug Enforcement Administration, and other members of the intelligence community fail under the pressure of networking. Professional relationships develop over years of attending the same meetings and conferences and manning joint task forces. Analysts share information, and eventually they share professional confidences that involve national secrets. In the end, there are no secrets, or at least very few secrets, between them. Ana Montes worked within the intelligence community for twenty-one years, first at the Department of Justice and then at DIA. Throughout that period of time, she networked. She was a master at the process of breaking down barriers to her access to classified information.

In recent years, another kind of networking, the interconnections between computer systems, has also broken down walls of silence and barriers to access. Computers have become the technical salvation of analysts—and the bane of counterintelligence types like me. Computers enable analysts to process information more efficiently and to share it as well. Information flows smoothly to the analysts, among the analysts, and between the analysts. That includes lots of information derived from secret sources and by secret means. The daily flow of information is staggering. There are mountains of it in our mainframes.

And now we have Intelink, a closed Internet-style system that makes finished reports quickly available to other members of the intelligence community. CIA analyses, DIA analyses, NSA products, and combatant command plans are all posted to Intelink. Once upon a time, bound reports were hand-carried only to the analysts who needed the information to accomplish their missions.

But with Intelink, anyone with authorized access to the system may view any product that has been posted to the system. A junior enlisted member of the armed forces assigned to an office in Japan can access finished intelligence reports from the CIA, DIA, NSA, or the National Geospatial-Intelligence Agency (NGA), on issues in Africa, Central America, the Middle East or Europe. An intelligence research specialist in Germany can view the daily intelligence briefing provided to the chairman of the Joint Chiefs of Staff moments after the chairman receives it. If an authorized Intelink user in Bogota, Colombia, wants to see the latest satellite photo of some obscure military base outside Kigali, Rwanda, it's available on the screen within an hour or so after the photo was snapped. The need-to-know principle no longer applies. Information simply flows.

The integration of intelligence information ensures that those who need it receive it in a timely fashion. That's a good thing. But the improvement was purchased at the cost of security. The increase in efficiency and broader access that such integration provides also increase the damage to national security if just one member of the intelligence community abuses that privilege of access, as Ana did.

The sheer volume of highly classified material available today simply boggles the mind, and it causes sleepless nights for counterintelligence guys like me. With the advent of shared computer systems, an analyst in Washington can electronically sift through tens of millions of pages of the government's most sensitive information to find those golden nuggets of information in which he or she has the greatest interest. For spies with the right clearance level, it's a candy store of information. Spies in Washington can use their computers to deliver tailor-made intelligence "take" to their foreign masters. There is no need to burden their handlers with piles of superfluous information, as American spies have done in the past.

Ana Montes enjoyed tremendous and deep access to the United States' secrets by virtue of her position at DIA. But perhaps her most valued access was to people, to colleagues within the intelligence community upon whom she could exercise influence.

Influence can be a subtle weapon. A word of encouragement here, a frown of doubt there—over time, its effect is equivalent to that of sprinkling drops of water on a rock, shaping it, even wearing it to dust. Conversely, influence can be wielded like an axe, eliminating contrary or contrasting views in a single, merciless chop. Ana had the knack for using influence however it proved necessary.

Ana exercised influence like few spies in U.S. history before her. She had the power to shape perceptions and to influence policy. Whenever members of Congress or their staffs queried the U.S. intelligence community about an issue related to Cuba, Ana authored DIA's response. On those occasions when the chairman of the Joint Chiefs of Staff provided testimony to Congress on issues related to Cuba, Ana drafted his remarks. Fidel Castro himself might as well have dictated our policy and positions concerning Cuba. Ana drafted NIEs and ICAs on Cuba. She was no ordinary intelligence analyst—and therefore no ordinary spy.

Ana also stayed at the Cuba desk at DIA for almost a decade. That's a long time for an analyst to remain on a single account. It's not unusual for an analyst to work continuously in a particular geographic region like Latin America for years on end. But to remain on a single account for a decade is somewhat unusual.

I suspect that Ana remained on the Cuba account for two basic reasons: It dovetailed nicely with her purely academic interest in Latin America and (the obvious) Cuban intelligence wanted her there. Her position on the account gave her direct access to the information in which her handlers had their greatest interest. Of equal importance to them, it also enabled her to build seniority and influence regarding her favorite subject, Cuba.

Other analysts in the intelligence community tended to rotate in and out over time. After a short stint on a Cuba account, for example, an analyst at some other agency would move on to some other country. His or her replacement would necessarily be junior in experience on the Cuba account to Ana Montes, the acknowledged expert throughout the community on issues pertaining to Cuba.

In time, whatever Ana had to say about Cuba was considered by other members of the intelligence community to be solid. True, she couldn't stray too far from reality in her analysis, because she had to support any position on any issue relative to Cuba with facts. But facts are subject to interpretation. Ana could, and did, exercise her prerogative as the senior expert in the community on Cuban political and military affairs to interpret facts as she chose. She could subtly spin, suggest, or ignore them. Her influence gave her other levers as well. For example, she could demand more data than was available before forming a judgment on any issue related to Cuba, or she could undermine a junior person's position or opinion, should it suit her purposes to do so. She was the queen of Cuba accounts, and everyone in her little world knew it.

Sticking with the Cuba account for a decade or so also gave Ana the ability to do something else that was equally powerful. She developed professional relationships with colleagues who, in time, advanced, moved into management, and sought jobs in other agencies where they rose to lofty positions.

One of these old friends, for example, had worked with Ana during the early 1990s. The same individual later served as the director for inter-American affairs at the National Security Council (NSC), formulating policy options on Latin America and Caribbean issues for presentation to the president through National Security Advisor (now Secretary of State) Condoleeza Rice. The director for inter-American affairs at the NSC, then, was an old colleague of Ana Belen Montes.

In the spring of 2001, while our investigation of Ana Montes was in progress, Ana and the DCI's national intelligence officer for Latin America met in the Old Executive Office Building next to the White House to brief the NSC on an issue related to Cuba in which Ana was recognizably a subject matter expert. Now that is influence in action.

Yet another former co-worker from the early 1990s rose to become the defense intelligence officer for Latin American affairs, the defense intelligence establishment's senior subject matter expert on Latin America. The DIO directly advises his boss, the director of military intelligence—the other hat worn by the DIA director. Although the CIA is more familiar to most Americans, the vast majority—perhaps two-thirds—of the intelligence community's multibillion dollar budget goes to the defense intelligence agencies. That means the DIO for Latin American affairs has major influence on the decision makers in our government. And he operated on a first-name basis with Ana, who served as his own subject-matter expert on Cuba.

Still another former colleague, a supervisor from the mid-1990s, rose to become the deputy assistant director for intelligence at DIA. It was he who nominated Ana for her promotion to the GG-14 pay grade. Ana Montes was golden, and these contacts formed a serious network for the exercise of her influence on behalf of Fidel Castro.

At the grass-roots level, Ana also maintained contact with Latin America specialists within every agency of the intelligence community. Over the years, those contacts moved like liquid throughout the community and academia and the plethora of think tanks that dot the landscape around the Beltway. Ana knew them all, and when she spoke to Cuba specialists in Washington, they listened.

And then, of course, there was Bill, Ana's boyfriend. My own gut-level assessment, as I wrote earlier, is that Ana was genuinely interested in their relationship on a personal level, and nothing more. But the skeptic within me believes that the Cuban Intelligence Service was fully aware of Bill and fully prepared to exploit that relationship. Bill was as innocent a dupe as there ever was, in my opinion. He did not know about Ana's involvement with Cuban intelligence. But he was about to get his hands, quite literally, on the United States' war plans at the time of Ana's arrest in September 2001.

Ana Montes was a perfect spy for Cuban intelligence. From her perch on the sixth floor of the DIAC, the intelligence community's queen of Cuba quietly gathered secrets to which she had authorized access and reached out to other members of the intelligence community, either to pump them for information or to influence their thoughts, opinions, and conclusions about Cuba.

In crisis situations, where a U.S. military response to Cuba might be contemplated, Ana Montes was one of the very first employees called into the Pentagon to advise and support the top brass. She was the perfect spy, right inside the Pentagon, watching our every move.

It was almost as though she had been born and raised in Havana, recruited into the clandestine service, and then given a false identity to enter the United States and get a job inside DIA. With her use of a shortwave radio, Ana was like the German spies operating in London during World War II with secret radios in their suitcases, posing as British citizens as they exchanged coded messages with Berlin. Except, of course, that Ana happened to be a U.S. citizen, born and bred. And in the morning, she went to work in the DIAC to find the information that her Cuban handlers had directed her to obtain for Cuba— information Cuba was likely to share with any number of associated states and organizations whose interests were inimical to those of the United States.

Maintaining that routine required extraordinary self-discipline, dedication, and commitment. Ana Montes was no ordinary spy. She was not in it for the money, or for the short haul. She was a master spy and, for Cuba, the perfect spy.

20

WHY SHE DID IT

I VISITED ANA'S CUBICLE ONE NIGHT during the investigation. My visit was lawful and to accomplish a specific task. But while I was there I paused to take in a sense of the place, to absorb the vibes, if you will. From experience, I knew that I could learn a lot about another human being by simply placing myself quietly within that person's space and noting my impressions.

Something was missing. I couldn't put my finger on it at first, but I soon realized that the cubicle was absolutely devoid of personality, of personal items. There were no pictures, photos, knick-knacks, birthday cards, or flowers, much less drawings or stuffed animals. The stuff of life, which most people use to decorate their work spaces, was simply not there. Ana either suffered from such low self-esteem that she deemed herself unworthy of a personal life or, more likely, she wished to prevent others from knowing her at all. I suspect she purposefully kept such items from her workplace in order to avoid the attention that such things tend to invite from others.

But looking closely, I did find something. And it may have been more telling about Ana and her motivation to spy than any number of photos or knickknacks. The walls of Ana's cubicle were, like so many others in the DIAC, covered with paperwork, tacked to her cubicle walls for quick and easy reference. Most of it was typed on standard 8-1/2-by-11-inch paper and rather neatly arrayed, one sheet closely aligned to the next across the walls. But on the wall that faced her computer monitor, at eye level and in plain view of anyone seated at her desk, a handwritten note caught my eye. It drew attention to itself, first, by its position on the wall. Unlike the other sheets of paper, the note was cockeyed, as though Ana had haphazardly pinned it to the wall in some haste. Upon close examination, I noted that it was in script, not typed, and that the ink appeared faded, as though it had been pinned to the wall for a long time. I read the words several times before the message sank in:

> The king hath note
> of all that they intend
> by interceptions
> which they dream not of.

I'm no literary scholar, but even I recognized the writing style of William Shakespeare when I first read those words. I had no idea which play it came from, or the context within which the words were spoken onstage. But I caught the gist of it anyway. My translation into modern-day English: The king is aware of their plans, and he developed his awareness of their plans by a secret and hidden means, the existence of which they cannot even imagine.

These could be the words of a spy or, variously, those of a counterspy. It depends upon the context. In fact, as I later learned, the passage was taken from act 2, scene 2 of Shakespeare's play *Henry V*. In the scene, members of the king's family are discussing traitors within the court. One is rattled and enraged by the fact that the king has allowed the traitors to continue their activity rather than simply arresting them. The other is calm and patient, noting that the arrests will be effected in time. The first speaker then acknowledges that the king is fully aware of everything that the traitors plan to do; moreover, the king has learned of their plans by a means that the traitors cannot even imagine.

Again, I'm no literary scholar. Shakespeare and I—well, we parted ways after I graduated from high school, and gladly. But I'm entitled to my opinion. And this is where I put my money: I believe that Ana held a very romantic and heroic view of her own role as a spy. She viewed herself as a heroine. The "king" in this passage—her passage—is, I believe, a reference to Fidel Castro. Not Uncle Sam.

I think that Ana twisted the context. If I am correct, then Ana Montes viewed herself as the "interceptions," the secret means by which Fidel Castro received all of Uncle Sam's plans. Castro was aware of all that Uncle Sam intended to do, and he was made aware of those plans by Ana the secret agent, whom Uncle Sam did not even suspect. My first reaction upon reading those words upon her wall was: Cool. It was as though I could look right into her heart. I understood from those words, intuitively, what drove her.

The beauty—the genius—of pinning that passage to her cubicle wall is pure Ana Montes because the passage can just as well be interpreted as a very patriotic statement. If challenged or even casually questioned by a passerby, Ana could reasonably explain that the "king" in the passage is a reference to Uncle Sam, that she is collecting information by secret means on his behalf against her target portfolio, Cuba, and that she pinned the passage to the wall to inspire her continued efforts. Pure genius, I think, and just like Ana, in that she always prepared an answer to any question, she anticipated every challenge, and she left nothing to chance.

Why did Ana Montes commit espionage? I have some ideas about her motives and her psyche. My ideas are drawn from years of experience in the business of dealing with people and, more specifically, from years of experience in the business of dealing with people who commit espionage. That said, I readily acknowledge that I cannot say exactly what drove Ana to spy. I haven't been inside her head. It's hard to say what, exactly, was going on in there. I'm not a psychiatrist.

Someone once created a handy acronym, MICE, to summarize the most common motivations for people who spy against their country. It stands for Money, Ideology, Coercion, and Ego. The idea is that people who spy do so for one or more of those reasons. Well, I've always felt that individuals in my business who have enough spare time and imagination on their hands to create this sort of thing ought to spend their energies more productively on the business of actually catching spies rather than on creating more acronyms. But MICE is a widely accepted acronym, so let's take a closer look and see how Ana Montes stacks up against it.

Money. For some spies, the problem is either need or greed; they need more money because they are in debt, or they greedily lust after more money than they can legally acquire. The solution to either problem, for people who are wired somewhat differently than you or me, and who have access to secret information, is to spy for cash. During the 1980s, the so-called Decade of the Spy, John Walker, James Hall, Jonathan Pollard, Ron Pelton, and many others were linked by a common thread—money. But we never found a hint that the Cubans paid Ana any money for her espionage, and there's no evidence she wanted them to. Besides, a more frugal and subdued life-style than that of Ana

Montes could not be imagined. She could teach the rest of us a thing or two about financial discipline. I have to conclude that money simply did not factor into Ana's decision to become a spy.

Ideology. Ideology is a body of doctrine that drives grand social or political movements. Doctrines like communism offer sweeping changes in relationships between human beings and promise to improve the quality of people's lives through political and social transformation. The opportunity to participate in such change, to "make a difference," can be a great motivator for spying, particularly for the romantics among us. But it has motivated very few Americans to commit espionage in recent years. I don't know why that is the case. During the 1930s, the 1940s, and the 1950s, a number of Americans spied for the Soviet Union out of a conviction that communism would save humanity by offering equity to everyone, creating a utopia. In their eyes, spying for the Soviet Union, therefore, was conducted for the benefit of all mankind. But spying for ideological reasons or out of political conviction seems to have fallen out of vogue for Americans after the height of the Cold War.

But not for Ana Montes. Certainly part of her motivation for spying was ideological. Like many other Americans, as she told me openly in our interview, she believed the U.S. approach to Cuba was counterproductive and oppressive. Ana was also Puerto Rican and was raised in a family that advocated achieving the political independence of Puerto Rico from the United States by peaceful means. The political independence of Puerto Rico is an emotional issue for many Puerto Ricans. Fidel Castro has often tried to play upon the sentiments of those who favor political independence by championing the cause of Puerto Rican independence against the oppressive Yankee colonizer of the north, presented as a mutual foe.

Ana Montes clearly viewed herself as a lonely heroine, willing to risk her freedom and her family's good name to serve the righteous cause of lifting oppression from the masses in secret league with her king, Fidel Castro. She was not an advocate of communism, but ideology was definitely part of this spy case.

Coercion. I'm not aware of any vulnerability in Ana's life that could have been exploited by use of blackmail. Besides, anyone who has spent any amount of time with Ana Montes can predict her likely response to an effort to force her cooperation: She'd laugh at the attempt. She could take care of herself. Some analysts employed by another federal agency said they actually feared her, though not because she would cause physical harm to anyone. Ana simply possessed a force of personality that was fearsome. She was one tough cookie who did not suffer fools gladly and offered no quarter in the face of opposition. During her arrest, she was pure ice. I can't picture Ana surrendering to blackmail or coercion. Nobody could have forced her to do anything that she didn't want to do.

Ego. Ego is a big motivator. I believe it played a major role in Ana's decision to step into the espionage arena and, more important, in her many decision points thereafter to continue to engage in espionage over a very long period of time.

In the MICE equation, "ego" refers to self-esteem and the emotional drivers that control behavior. Often, events and situations which occur early in life, during childhood, imprint themselves heavily upon the psyche and serve to influence a person's day-to-day behavior until death. For example, a person who grows up poor may develop a psychological "need" for more money that is never satisfied, regardless of the amount of money that he or she accumulates during a lifetime of employment. The perpetual need for ever greater amounts of money is perceived, not real, but for the individual, it is just as urgent.

Those who commit espionage are driven to do so in order to satisfy very personal, and perceived, psychological needs. They discover that the act of espionage at least temporarily satisfies those needs. Thus someone who feels unappreciated at work may become a spy in order to "get even" with a supervisor who has treated him or her unfairly. Someone who feels small and inconsequential in life can transform himself into a Big Man on Campus in the eyes of foreign intelligence handlers—he can become a very important person, indeed, to them. Perceived needs carry the weight of reality inside a spy's head.

What was Ana's need? And what drove her to attach so much weight to satisfying that need that she was willing to risk her reputation, her career, her freedom, and the well-being of her family and friends? What was so important?

I struggled throughout the investigation to understand what drove Ana Montes to spy against her country. The Shakespearean quote that I found pinned to her cubicle wall offered a hint: Ana viewed herself as some kind of secret champion for Fidel Castro, and she delighted in that role. Later, prior to sentencing, Ana herself offered an explanation: She was morally outraged by the U.S. government's policies toward Nicaragua and Cuba, policies which caused harm to poor innocents and served to oppress them. Ana viewed herself as their heroine, someone who sacrificed herself on their behalf against a bullying northern neighbor, the United States.

Hers was a seemingly noble cause, and I am certain that she reveled in it. But what caused such rage within this young woman that she felt compelled to act in a manner that most of us consider to be irrational, irresponsible, and unlawful? After all, many people disagree with the policies the United States follows in its dealings with Cuba. U.S. senators and congressmen are among those who feel strongly that our approach to Cuba is counterproductive, even wrong. But they don't commit espionage to right the wrong. Ana did so. Why?

Spying for Cuba was important to her. It satisfied a deep and very personal need. What drove such rage? What happened to this young woman, perhaps early in her life, to create such a need within her? Why was Ana Montes so angered by the effect that U.S. government policies had, or were perceived to have, upon the Nicaraguan and Cuban people that she felt compelled to insert herself as their savior?

The answer to that question began to surface during the course of the investigation. Among Ana's writings were references to abuse that she and her siblings had suffered at the hands of a domineering father and the deep-seated guilt that Ana continued to feel for not protecting her younger and weaker siblings from his bullying. Ana was the oldest child, and she naturally felt responsible in part for their safety and well-being. As she saw it, she'd failed them. She should have done more. And she never forgave herself for failing to intervene and spare them from someone she viewed as an abusive bully.

Guilt is a powerful motivator. It drives each of us and our behaviors, in unconscious ways, throughout our lives. A child who steals candy from a convenience store may feel shame for the rest of his or her life, and the resulting guilt may drive a lifelong obsession for meticulously lawful behavior into old age. Failure to save a playmate from injury or death can drive a child to pursue employment as a doctor, a nurse, or any other profession that he or she views as helpful, even life-saving. Childhood experiences affect us in both positive and negative ways, and they sometimes mar us forever.

Was the abuse that Ana and her siblings suffered at the hands of their late father really all that bad? Perhaps not. Ana's siblings and mother offer differing views and different recollections of family dynamics and specific events that occurred within the Montes household while Ana was growing up. One person's strict and unbending discipline may be another person's abuse, and it would be unfair to Ana's father to label him as an abusive person if he was not. But that's hardly the point. What matters is the effect that his disciplinary actions had upon Ana.

Ana grew up to be a self-perceived heroine who sacrificed herself on behalf of a weak and seemingly helpless group of people who suffered at the hands of a bullying northern neighbor. She would accept no money or other compensation for doing so. After all, hers was a noble cause. She may have been unable to protect her younger, weaker siblings from their father during their childhood, and she continued to suffer from guilt for that "failure" throughout her life. But she made up for it. She became a heroine in Havana. And that must be quite an ego trip.

Whatever the motivation to commit espionage, it must satisfy a deep-seated psychological need within the spy. When espionage occurs voluntarily, without coercion, strong emotional drivers must work to overcome the usual inhibitions that keep most of us from even considering a commission of the act.

My job at DIA is a mission. It is more than just a job. It is a serious, focused, single-minded pursuit of spies within our agency. And I am driven.

But my drive and focus as a mole hunter pale by comparison to the drive and focus exhibited by Ana Montes as a spy. The reality is that while I have spent the last twenty years or so on a simple professional mission, Ana Montes spent her time at DIA on a crusade. She was a true believer, out to slay the dragon.

21

HOW SHE GOT AWAY WITH IT

HOW DID ANA MONTES GET AWAY WITH IT? First, we must give the Cubans their due. They ran a highly placed agent under our noses for many years without detection. That's not an easy task. It required the disciplined employment of espionage tradecraft that has been designed, tested, and proven through years of practice to deny U.S. counterintelligence the ability to discover their agents. It worked.

It shouldn't surprise us that the Cubans were capable of running such an operation successfully. After all, Cuba has been closely aligned for several decades with the Soviets, and later the Russians, the acknowledged masters of human intelligence, who continue to be perhaps the very best in the business. We may assume that the Cuban intelligence officers selected to run Ana's operation were trained by Russian experts and that Ana's controllers were among the best Cuba had to offer.

The reality is, the Cuban Intelligence Service has been kicking our butts in the intelligence business for decades. We've underestimated them. They've scammed us, they've tied up our resources on worthless, controlled operations, and they've essentially run circles around us since Fidel Castro first gained control of the island. The FBI's success in 1998 against Cuba's Wasp network in Miami notwithstanding, the U.S. record of success against Cuban intelligence operations has been dismal. Ana Montes was the first major Cuban spy caught by the FBI since Castro came to power in 1959.

And yet we continue to underestimate the Cubans. Not long after the Montes investigation, I expressed my concerns to a seasoned U.S. counter-intelligence professional. To my surprise, he dismissed my concern that Cuban intelligence might be more sophisticated and more expert than many in U.S. counterintelligence had earlier imagined. He scoffed, "But Scott, it's just a little island." It was as though the physical size of the place and its population were measures of Cuba's ability to steal U.S. secrets! I'm sorry, but there is no such correlation.

We must give Ana Montes her due, too. She did some things very well. First, she maintained a low profile and avoided the attention of the DIA security office and the FBI for many years—no extravagant expenditures, no flashy cars, no questionable work after hours or on the weekends. She did little to draw attention to herself.

During my first eight years on the job at DIA, I never so much as heard her name in any context. For all intents and purposes, our security office did not know her. She simply did not come up on our scope until 1996. No security violations, no security infractions, no questionable or suspicious behavior was attributed to her. She just came into work every day on time, did her work, and then left for home at the end of the day.

Starting in 1989, DIA's security office launched a significant effort to raise the counterintelligence awareness of DIA employees through a briefing program we called DICE, for Defensive Information to Counter Espionage. The Decade of the Spy, the 1980s, had just concluded, and DIA's security managers realized a need for a proactive program to protect the Agency from foreign agents operating within its walls. The primary objective of DICE was to encourage co-workers to report suspicions or concerns about their fellow employees to the security office. That's a hard sell to make in the United States, as I've mentioned, but an energetic and charismatic security employee named Ray Semko did a fine job of it. Lots of employees reported lots of concerns about lots of other employees. For years, not one of them stepped forward to report suspicions about Ana Montes. It was not until 1996 that a DICE briefing prompted a DIA employee, Reg Brown, to report any concerns about her.

Of equal significance was Ana's ability to win the trust and confidence of her superiors. She performed superbly in that regard. It's hard for any supervisor to develop negative thoughts, much less suspicions, about an outstanding employee who makes the supervisor look good at every turn by consistently churning out outstanding work products—especially one who is happy to step aside and allow the supervisor to share the credit. Ana Montes was a star. What supervisor in his or her right mind would run to the security office to point a finger of suspicion at his best employee? Ana's good attitude and effort at work shielded her from any suspicion that might otherwise arise.

Then there's the question of the polygraph. Ana submitted to a DIA-administered counterintelligence scope polygraph examination in March 1994, and she beat it. She passed. The Cubans have an established track record of training agents to defeat polygraph examinations. Ana was just one of many who have done so.

I am not a polygraph examiner. I cannot explain how she managed to defeat our exam. But I can speak with some authority about the level of credence that investigators assign to polygraph results.

Those of us who work most intimately with the examiners understand that the test is not infallible. True, we like the polygraph. It is a great tool for investigators. I believe it serves as a deterrent to most spies, or would-be spies, who consider penetrating our agency, and it is most useful as a tool to support our favorite and most effective investigative technique, the interview. Still, investigators are fully aware of the fact that the polygraph can be beaten, particularly by those who are trained by experts to do so. We never rely solely on polygraph results as an indicator of a person's past behavior.

If polygraph results could stand alone, we wouldn't bother to conduct general background investigations and more specific security investigations on our employees, as we do. We'd simply polygraph every employee, continuously, and be done with it. So while test results are certainly factored into the decision-making process, they are never the only indicator of an employee's suitability for access to classified information.

Polygraph results may be used by some in the decision whether to grant access to an employee or in judging whether an employee may have committed an offense, but only after weighing other suitability indicators and behavioral factors. Then, if the call is a close one, the trump card of the polygraph is sometimes played: "Well, she *did* pass her polygraph examination, so, all other factors being equal, she appears to be good to go."

Still, I wish I could tell you how she defeated that exam. And then, of course, we missed some indicators that she did exhibit during the early years of her employment with DIA. For example: She lied. In fact, she lied about two things when we first hired her. Lying is an integrity issue; it could have been used to eliminate her from consideration during the hiring process, had we known of it then, or when we reexamined her suitability for access to classified information. Instead, we overlooked the lies when they came to light. We rationalized them away.

At the time we hired Ana in 1985, we asked her about past drug use. She admitted to some minor use of marijuana and cocaine when she was in college. Such experimentation, in which all too many American kids participate, especially at that age, is driven by peer pressure, curiosity, and wanting to fit into the in-crowd. Ana said that she had last used drugs in 1979, while she was an undergraduate at the University of Virginia and before she accepted employment with the Department of Justice as a FOIA paralegal. That was not true.

We know that because she corrected the story herself years later. She voluntarily admitted to us that she had used cocaine on a few occasions in 1982 while employed by the Justice Department, while she had a Top Secret security clearance. There are many reasons why an employee might volunteer such information. It's possible that someone else was going to report the matter to security anyway, so she simply jumped the gun and self-reported it. There are other possibilities, too, but her motivation in reporting the lie is not relevant to my point here. The bottom line is, she lied, and we let her get away with it.

She lied on another issue, too. On one of her application forms for employment with DIA, Ana indicated that she had received a master's degree from Johns Hopkins University upon completion of her coursework in 1984. The truth was, Ana owed a couple of thousand dollars to the school for a tuition loan. The school withheld the degree pending receipt of her payment. So technically, she had not yet received the degree when she completed her application in 1985. Another lie, but again, we let it slide. The lies were relatively minor and they were easily rationalized by the security office.

Ana informed us about these lies in 1991. That's six years after she came on board with the agency. By then, she had established herself as a superior employee, earning outstanding and distinguished performance evaluations year after year. In 1991, she was accepted into the DCI's Exceptional Analyst Program, giving her a year to study a topic of her choice while receiving her federal salary. Her supervisors already thought the world of Ana Montes. A couple of little white lies were easily forgiven.

Still another issue surfaced early in her career with DIA—loyalty. The issue was raised by a former co-worker at the DOJ who stated in 1985, during Ana's initial security background investigation with the DoD, that Ana Montes had voiced her disagreement with the U.S. government's policy toward Cuba. When pressed, the former co-worker would not suggest that Ana was disloyal, and she expressed doubt that Ana would ever compromise classified information. But the former co-worker felt uncomfortable enough about Ana's deep-seated disagreement with the U.S. government that she made an issue of it during the background investigation.

Now, we did follow up on this one. Ana was challenged on three occasions—including my interview with her in 1996—to account for her disagreement with the U.S. government's policy toward Cuba. Each time she provided the best of answers: It was true. She *did* disagree with the U.S. government's policy and approach toward Cuba. It had been ineffective and even counterproductive in its effort to bring democracy to the Cuban people. But— and this is a big "but"—she noted that it was her right as a U.S. citizen to disagree with her government. A lot of people do. She disagreed with the policy, and yet, she claimed, she remained a loyal American who had never done anything to harm the United States. It was the perfect answer, wrapped in the U.S. flag.

So what were we to do with a U.S. citizen, who happened to be a DIA analyst, who disagreed with government policy? It was her right to disagree. Although those of us in the security field might be uncomfortable with an employee who disagrees with government policy on any issue, the fact is, we could not tar and feather her. We had to let it go.

This business of mole hunting can be difficult and frustrating. It's a bit like trying to find ghosts in a fog. The only indication of their presence may be a vapor trail, and that's not much to go on.

I do wish that spies would paint great big glowing, gooey blobs on their foreheads for easy identification. Green ones, perhaps. It would certainly make my job much easier. But spies do not do that. Ana Montes certainly didn't. She simply slipped through the fog, never calling attention to herself for a moment. And so she got away with espionage for a long time.

22

WHY IT MATTERS

SINCE THE FALL OF THE BERLIN WALL and the end of the Cold War, I've sensed an increasingly blasé attitude among the American people toward the crime of espionage. Now that the Cold War is over and the threat of instant immolation by a Soviet nuclear attack is no longer credible, it seems that we view spying as an anachronism, a meaningless game played by fogies of the past, as though espionage were of no consequence or relevance to the modern era. Unfortunately, nothing could be further from the truth.

The world is a dangerous place, and we are sending our youth into it. U.S. military forces are engaged in activities in more locations around the world than at almost any other time in the nation's history. And not everybody out there likes us. We need to support those kids, so they can make it back home alive and in one piece. We don't need someone to stab them in the back by stealing, or failing to protect, secrets that may be vital to their safety. They're in enough danger already.

I've got three kids of my own, all boys. If any of them comes to harm because of the traitorous actions of some future Ana Montes, well, I won't be happy. That's why espionage matters. As for the Ana Montes case, here's a sample of what could have happened while Ana was on watch at DIA. Let me be clear. What I've listed below are the obvious occasions for potential damage, the clear risks that existed during the period she was a Cuban agent. I can't state that she and the Cubans took advantage of each one of these openings, although they had the opportunity. Nor can I prove that Montes was responsible for the loss of American lives in combat. But decide for yourself.

El Salvador and Nicaragua

Ana Montes was the DIA's principal analyst for El Salvador and Nicaragua in the late 1980s, her first years at the agency. She knew more about the military situation in those countries than virtually anyone else in the United States. It so happens that the United States and Cuba were fighting, in effect, a proxy war in the region at that time. In El Salvador, the United States supported the government against the rebel FMLN forces; in Nicaragua, it supported the Contra rebels against the Sandinista government. The United States had troops on the ground in El Salvador, working as military advisors and trainers for the Salvadoran army. More than twenty young U.S. military men died in that conflict. In Nicaragua, it's possible that some Americans assisted the Contra rebels in the field, although I have no knowledge of such activity. Anything's possible.

Meanwhile, according to local and regional media, the Cubans were providing arms and support to the FMLN in their fight against the Salvadoran government. Both Cuba and Nicaragua also openly declared that more than a thousand Cuban military advisors were in Nicaragua to train, support, and advise the Nicaraguan military against the Contras. The Cubans denied, however, that any of their troops—many of whom were combat veterans from a jungle war raging in Angola since the mid-1970s—operated in the field in support of Nicaraguan forces.

Confusing, isn't it? The point is, U.S. troops were in the field, the Cubans were supporting our adversaries in the field, and Ana Montes, already a Cuban agent, was in a position to tell the Cubans everything the U.S. government knew about the military situation on the ground in El Salvador and Nicaragua. Ana's knowledge of the size, structure, disposition, status, and plans of the Salvadoran military, along with the size, structure, disposition, status, and plans of the U.S. forces in El Salvador—some of them Special Forces operating in the field—was encyclopedic. Her knowledge of Nicaraguan forces, the Contra rebels facing them, and U.S. efforts to support the Contras was equally in-depth.

The chief of Nicaraguan intelligence during that time was a Cuban officer. We can only speculate whether he received any special help from Havana as a result of information received from Cuba's agents within the U.S. government—

or whether Ana Montes provided information to the Cubans that ultimately led to the deaths of U.S. troops or contractors in El Salvador or Nicaragua. More on this one in my final chapter.

Panama

In 1989, U.S. forces jumped into Panama to apprehend General Manuel Noriega, to disarm and disband the Panama Defense Forces, and to restore political stability to the region in defense of the U.S. strategic interest in maintaining the viability of the Panama Canal. But the operation didn't go quite as well as planned. Twenty-three of our boys were killed in action or died later from wounds suffered in action, and many more were wounded. U.S. Navy Seals were trapped in the open on the airport tarmac while attempting to disable Noriega's personal aircraft. Army Rangers and airborne troops suffered heavy casualties because the Panama Defense Forces had been placed on alert and were waiting for our combat troops as they floated to the ground.

Noriega received word of the action more than a week before the first U.S. troops landed. Rumor had it that Cuba's signals intelligence site at Lourdes had intercepted telephone conversations between U.S. general officers back in the States, alerting the Cubans to planned troop movements in advance. That's quite possible. It is also possible that the Cubans planted that rumor to cover the fact that they had actually received information from an inside source, a spy in Washington. There is a lot that I don't know. But Cuba's interests in Panama did not mirror our own; they did not want us there. Does anyone doubt that Cuba would have alerted Manuel Noriega to an impending U.S. attack if it learned of it?

Ana Montes did not provide intelligence support to war planners for Operation Just Cause. Her assignment at the time was Nicaragua and El Salvador, not Panama, so the plans for the invasion would not have automatically come across her desk. On the other hand, as a cleared DIA Latin America specialist, she could have gained access to them if she chose to do so. Again, I don't know that Ana Montes said a word to the Cubans about U.S. military plans, intentions, or movements toward Panama. Perhaps she didn't. My point is simply this: Here is one more real-life occasion when a spy in Ana's position could easily have caused damage with life-or-death results. Espionage does matter.

Cuban Émigrés and Opponents of the Castro Regime

Ana Montes was also in a position to harm Cubans, both in and out of Cuba—and particularly those opposed to Castro's regime and sympathetic to U.S. aims. While I don't expect many Americans to shed tears over those losses, I suspect that some Americans, especially those whose relatives remain in Cuba, may feel otherwise.

Many Cubans serving in the government or the military fled their country during the sixteen years that Ana was actively spying for Cuba, from 1985 to 2001. Upon reaching the United States, some may have volunteered statements in which they identified other officials and military officers in Cuba who had grown tired or disillusioned with Castro's regime. Ana would have routinely read such reports and could easily have passed those names along to her Cuban handlers. Did the Cuban government take action against officials and officers named in those reports? I wonder about their relatives, too. Could Ana have Cuban blood on her hands? I don't know.

Operations Desert Shield and Desert Storm

I remember arriving at work at the DIA every morning during Operation Desert Shield, the build-up to Desert Storm. The United States was shipping the equivalent of a mid-sized city to Saudi Arabia, using every ship and plane it could find. Every morning, I'd fire up my computer and read the daily sit-rep, the situation report that tallied every bean, bullet, and body bag being shipped to the Persian Gulf. It was absolutely amazing. The daily sit-rep typically ran to one hundred pages. At the time, the very existence of F-117A stealth fighters was a big secret, but we were flying them to the gulf region in advance of the offensive. The sit-rep provided their numbers and their final destinations. Everything that we were throwing into the gulf was detailed in those reports. Ana certainly had access to those reports. I wonder now whether she read them, too.

It wasn't just the sit-reps. All kinds of intelligence reporting was being created back then. Mini–task forces were formed and mid-range and longer-term analytical teams studied a variety of what-if scenarios. One such task force was located right on the sixth floor at the DIAC, just around the corner from Ana's cubicle.

Ana was not directly involved in planning and support for the Gulf War. Her expertise lay in Latin America. But she had access. And the Cubans? Well, they were not exactly supportive of Desert Shield or Desert Storm. We can only imagine whether they might have provided information to the Iraqi regime, if they had acquired any information of value to Saddam Hussein. I have no information to suggest that Ana Montes passed information about our plans or details of our build-up along to her Cuban masters. Still, communications between Ana and her Cuban handlers throughout Desert Shield and Desert Storm were heavy, and Ana was certainly in a great position to access insider information that was of interest to Cuba and to countries with which Castro was aligned.

Operation Uphold Democracy

In 1994, U.S. forces were sent to Haiti to support President Jean-Bertrand Aristide following an attempted coup by his political rivals. An intelligence task force focused intelligence support on the subject for U.S. policymakers.

Even though Aristide was a socialist, Cuba strongly opposed what it saw as U.S. interference in its own region, the Caribbean. The cornerstone of Cuba's foreign policy remained the belief that the United States would one day invade Cuba and topple its government. Fidel Castro, his brother Raul, and other senior Cuban leaders openly stated to the media that they thought the use of military force in Haiti to calm social unrest was simply an attempt by the United States to establish a precedent. They believed the United States planned to follow up by fomenting unrest in Cuba, giving it an excuse to invade.

Where was Ana? As the DIA's top Cuba analyst, she was a member of the intelligence task force on Haiti, of course. But she was not just any member of that task force. Ana later received a Special Act Award for drafting an information paper for the Office of the Joint Chiefs of Staff and the Office of the Secretary of Defense. The paper was then presented to the National Security Council as it crafted policy for the White House on targeting sanctions against violators of the Governor's Island accord, the agreement between Aristide and those who had ousted him that mandated his return. Castro's agent had drafted the basis for White House policy. *That* is influence.

As usual, Ana also had direct access to the intelligence that supported U.S. troops in the field. She knew what they were doing, what they were going to do, and when and how they were going to do it. I assume, therefore, that Fidel Castro knew all of that, as well.

The Cuban Shootdown of Brothers to the Rescue Aircraft

We've pretty well covered this incident, in which the Cuban military shot down two civilian aircraft in international airspace, killing all four aboard. But it serves as such an excellent example of what a spy can accomplish for another country and against the interests of the United States that I feel compelled to mention it again. Ana Montes was in a position to influence decision making and to provide false or skewed information directly to the decision makers in the offices of the Joint Chiefs of Staff that day. Had the United States decided to respond militarily, she was also in the perfect position to warn Cuba in advance and provide every detail of the plan. Had the men and women of our armed forces participated directly in any such attack, their lives would certainly have been placed in great peril as the Cubans prepared for their arrival.

Plan Colombia

During the summer of 2001, Ana Montes prepared to relinquish the Cuban account to another analyst at DIA during her planned absence on her year-long NIC fellowship. Ana's supervisors decided they would place her on the Colombia account when she came back to the agency . It may be pure coincidence that the latest focus of Cuba's attention at that time was also Colombia— specifically, Plan Colombia, the U.S. initiative to support the government of Colombia in its fight against drug traffickers. As I mentioned earlier, rumor had it that the Cubans opposed Plan Colombia. In fact, rumor had it that the Cubans were supporting rebel forces arrayed against the government of Colombia, once again pitting Cuban military interests against those of the United States.

U.S. Special Forces troops were in Colombia to train members of the Colombian military. Technical advisors were there to assist in maintaining U.S.-manufactured equipment and in training Colombian forces to maintain it. As a Colombia analyst, of course, Ana Montes would have had full access to everything that the United States military was doing in Colombia. Who could doubt that she would have turned all of that information over to her Cuban handlers, and that Havana would have exploited that information to our detriment in Colombia? I'm sure that our Special Forces troops in Colombia are happy to know that Ana has been removed from the scene—as are their spouses, children, parents, friends, siblings, aunts, and uncles.

The War on Terrorism

It's a good thing we stopped her in time. Cuba is not our friend. Fidel Castro opposes the United States' current counterterrorism initiative. He's aligned with some states that may support, sponsor, or harbor terrorists, or have done so in the recent past. In the months preceding the September 11 attacks, Castro toured Syria, Libya, and Iran. While in Iran, he crystallized his goals regarding the United States when he said, "Iran and Cuba, in cooperation with each other, can bring America to its knees." If Ana Montes were still operating at DIA, it would not be beneath or beyond Fidel Castro or his successors to share information received from her with those countries and other supporters of international terrorism.

Of course, this particular window of opportunity never opened for Ana Montes. At the time of her arrest, she was about to gain access to many details of our preparations for war in Afghanistan—virtually everything. Fortunately, we could arrest her before that happened.

23

THE DEATH OF A WARFIGHTER

THE MEDIA PAID SCANT ATTENTION to the Ana Montes story at the time of her arrest and eventual conviction. Bigger stories dominated the news during the fall of 2001, and in any event, spying for Cuba seemed relatively inconsequential.

But any time the media informs us that an American has committed the most heinous of crimes, the crime of espionage, we should push the media and our government to answer the most obvious of questions: Did anyone die? Because that is the worst consequence of the crime. Other damage to national security may occur, and does, but the death of American warfighters is the ultimate measure of a spy's depravity. We should know about death when it occurs.

In the case of Ana Montes, someone did die. His name was Gregory A. Fronius, and his story can now be told in its proper context.

To be fair, Ana Montes was not solely responsible for Greg's death. Other spies were at work when Greg died, and they likely contributed more directly to his death than did Montes. But she was there. She was involved. And she chose to stand against a warfighter rather than support him, as she was sworn to do. She therefore shares responsibility for his death. At the very least, she stood on the wrong side of the fence when he died.

Some time after Ana's conviction, the National Counterintelligence Executive (NCIX) was tasked to conduct a damage assessment of her espionage. As part of that assessment, NCIX asked DIA and the FBI whether Ana was responsible for the deaths of any U.S. military members. I conducted some research to answer that question, and that is how I stumbled upon Greg's story. My initial sources of information were some old newspaper reports and a couple of after-action reports that were written by the Department of Defense. In writing this chapter, I also contacted Greg's brothers and their families, his wife and kids, and a few other knowledgeable people in order to gather some more information about who Greg was as a person. Although he is gone, I wanted to get to know him as well as I could—not just as a faceless statistic, but as a human being.

For me, this story is a reminder of the ultimate reason for my work, the terrible price that U.S. service members and their families risk paying every day to preserve our freedoms. Whatever I can do, or DIA can do, to support warfighters like Greg—and bring them home alive—we will do. In the best sense of the term, we, not people like Ana Montes, are the real "true believers." Our mission is to make sure stories like this don't happen again.

I begin with the end of the story. Gregory A. Fronius was killed in action in El Salvador in the early morning hours of May 31, 1987. He was a Green Beret, one of America's finest warfighters. He was an expert in the use of small arms and in the execution of small unit tactics. His job was to train members of the Salvadoran armed forces, with a view toward increasing their combat capability.

I mentioned the Special Forces mission in El Salvador in the previous chapter. Their role was critical to the success of the U.S. policy to contain and reverse the spread of communism in Central America. In 1979, the Marxist-oriented Sandinistas, supported by Cuba, had gained control of Nicaragua. As I noted earlier, a Cuban general officer was appointed to establish and run Nicaragua's fledgling intelligence service. President Ronald Reagan chose to support a reactive insurgency known as the Contras to retake control of the government from the Sandinistas.

Meanwhile, in the neighboring country of El Salvador, a coalition of Marxist political parties was laying siege to the democratically elected government in a guerrilla insurgency. The rebel FMLN forces waged an incessant and bloody military campaign throughout the 1980s, supported by both Nicaragua and Cuba. The United States provided military training and support to the Salvadoran armed forces in their battle against the FMLN. That's where Greg

Fronius and approximately fifty additional members of the U.S. Special Forces entered the picture.

Members of the U.S. Special Forces are extraordinary men. They share a mental toughness that enables them to single-mindedly focus upon accomplishing difficult missions under the most hazardous of conditions. They are winners, and only the finest are chosen to join their ranks. Greg Fronius was one of them.

I asked Greg's brother Anthony what we should know about Greg. Anthony answered without hesitation, "Greg Fronius was a patriot. He loved this country." He added, "We used to tease Greg because he was born on Election Day—November 3, 1959—and Greg was such a flag-waving kind of guy." That was the day John F. Kennedy was elected president. Greg was also, by all accounts, a carefree and colorful spirit. He was a playful, red-haired, and freckled all-American kid. He loved to climb trees, wrestle in the yard with his brothers, go camping, and swing like Tarzan from the rope swings his brothers would hang over the river near home. Later on, those activities gave way to playing loud music (1950s and 1960s rock and roll was his favorite), driving fast, playing practical jokes on his friends and family, and chasing girls. "He wasn't just the life of the party," his sister-in-law Darlene told me, "Greg *was* the party!" He ran the show, and he was a popular guy.

Greg was the youngest of three brothers born in Plainsville, Ohio. His dad died when Greg was about nine years old. Mom remarried, and the family shuttled back and forth between Plainsville and southwest Pennsylvania until finally settling down in Connellsville, Pennsylvania, when Greg was about fifteen.

As the youngest of three boys, Greg grew up tough. He and his oldest brother Steve used to play Army in a local junkyard. "Greg always played to win," Steve recalled. Warfare was, after all, a serious business. They used glass bottles as hand grenades, tossing them in earnest at each other. The explosions of glass fragments were proof against the familiar shouted claims of childhood battles: "You missed me!" Greg didn't miss. Family members already knew that someday Greg Fronius would become a soldier. He was made for it.

In high school, Greg went out for wrestling, and he loved it. "Greg would come home after school and draw a big circle in the yard," Darlene told me, "and then he'd take on all comers. I can still picture him out there." The last thing you ever wanted to do was to injure Greg Fronius. Steve recalled a time when he and Greg were wrestling in the house. Things got out of hand, as they often do with brothers. Furniture crashed, the couch overturned, and a coffee table lay practically in splinters. Then Steve heard the crack of Greg's fingers, and he backed away for fear of causing further injury.

Not so Greg. His response was more like that of a wounded animal. Steve took the brunt of Greg's wounded wrath that day, as he vividly recalls. It was emblematic of the indomitable spirit that Greg would exhibit during the final fight of his life. He simply refused to lose.

Greg joined the Army in 1977. He was eighteen years old. Everyone who knew him believed that he would someday join the Special Forces. "Greg's favorite movies were *The Blues Brothers*—because he loved the music—and *The Green Berets*, starring John Wayne," Anthony recalled. Greg always laughed at the "Provo's Privy" scene in *The Green Berets*, in which a building at Fort Bragg is named after a fallen Green Beret. It's an amusing scene, meant to evoke nervous laughter from the audience through a little black humor.

But his favorite part of the movie, contrary to what one might expect of the macho image of the Special Forces, was the last scene, in which John Wayne walks quietly onto the beach with a young Vietnamese boy. The boy has just lost his favorite Green Beret, a casualty of combat, and he is both saddened by his loss and frightened for his own future. He looks up to John Wayne and asks, "Who is going to take care of me now?" Wayne places a hand on the boy's shoulder and responds, "We will, son"—meaning that the Green Berets would take care of him. It is a tear-jerker of a scene. It was Greg's favorite because it spoke to him about the core mission of the Green Berets, whose motto, "De Oppresso Liber," means "To free and protect the oppressed." Greg viewed the Green Berets not as the macho commandos of Hollywood's "Rambo"-style films but as the quiet professionals they are in reality.

During his early years in the Army, Greg was assigned to a unit in Panama, where in 1981 he met his future wife, Celinda. She was a university student in Panama employed by a local Panamanian company. They met at a dance.

"There was nothing shy about Greg," Celinda later recalled. He didn't speak a word of Spanish, and Celinda's English was limited to a few words. But that didn't stop Greg from courting her. His natural confidence won her heart. He also charmed her family. "Greg was fun," Celinda explained. "My mother and brothers just fell in love with him." Greg and Celinda soon married, and their first child—Greg Junior—was born later that year.

In 1983, Greg completed the Army's rigorous Special Forces training at Fort Bragg, North Carolina. Next, he studied for a year at the Defense Language

Institute in Monterey, California, the same place where I learned Mandarin Chinese back in 1970. Greg was there to study Spanish in preparation for his assignment to the 7th Special Forces Group, then based in Panama.

Typically for him, Greg made new friends in Panama quickly. "I think he knew more people in Panama than I did," Celinda told me. "Greg could never just sit down somewhere. He was always jogging and lifting weights." Every spare moment, she said, was spent with Greg Junior. "Greg was really good with kids. He was always taking them somewhere—to the beach or downtown. Wherever he went, Greg Junior went along."

In 1985, a second child joined the family. Francine was just a toddler when Greg died, so she has no memory of him. Today Francine soaks up stories about her father like a sponge.

I sat in her mother's kitchen one day and told Francine a story about her father. I had heard it from Doug Vander Pool, a fellow Green Beret. During their assignment in Panama, members of the 3rd Battalion of the 7th Special Forces Group were parachuting from helicopters at a height of ten thousand feet. As he stood to position himself for the jump, Doug's parachute prematurely deployed. The wind caught the chute and threatened to yank him from the helicopter to a certain death. Acting instinctively, Greg quickly wrapped his arms around Doug's body and pulled him into the helicopter to safety, saving his life. Doug felt a debt of gratitude, but Greg, typically, just shrugged it off. He had simply done what had to be done.

In January 1987, Greg was assigned to the 4th Infantry Brigade of the Salvadoran Armed Forces (ESAF). He was stationed at the 4th IB's headquarters compound in a place called El Paraiso—in English, Paradise. The compound was about as far from a true paradise as one might imagine.

El Paraiso was in the heart of FMLN-controlled territory, about thirty miles east of the capital city of San Salvador. The compound had been built by Green Berets earlier in the war, and the ESAF considered it impregnable. It was a fortress and a showpiece. When foreign dignitaries visited El Salvador, they commonly toured the 4th IB's compound at El Paraiso, presented as an example of El Salvador's military might and a symbol of its determination to prevail. Located as it was in the FMLN's back yard, the 4th IB's compound at El Paraiso was also a thorn in the side of the FMLN and a priority target for enemy attack. There was reason to believe that such an attack was imminent.

Greg Fronius was one of only three Green Berets assigned to support the 4th IB. His job was to provide basic infantry training to ESAF troops. Under the rules of engagement, he couldn't even leave the compound except to provide training for ESAF forces or to provide humanitarian relief to the local citizenry. He was not allowed to patrol or to engage in any combat operation, short of self-defense. Greg Fronius was an American warfighter. But this was someone else's war, and Greg's mission in El Salvador was to train ESAF troops, not to go into battle alongside them.

The compound served as a base of operations for approximately two thousand ESAF soldiers. Most of them spent their time securing transportation routes against FMLN efforts to disrupt the fragile Salvadoran economy, patrolling roads and securing bridges. These were purely defensive operations. But a small contingent of Salvadoran Special Forces also based in the compound engaged in offensive operations, disrupting FMLN military operations in the district by attacking and killing as many FMLN rebels as possible. Offensive operations by these Special Forces late in 1986 and early in 1987 were very successful. But the FMLN had a few cards up their sleeves—trump cards, in fact, in the form of collaborators or infiltrators located inside the compound at El Paraiso.

The 4th IB's compound at El Paraiso, the impregnable fortress of the Salvadoran Armed Forces, was in reality quite vulnerable to enemy attack. Its vaunted security posture, which consisted of multiple layers of mine fields, barbed wire, and various other defensive measures typical of a U.S. Special Forces base camp, had a hollow center—ESAF troops recruited by FMLN guerrillas to betray the camp. Their recruitment was facilitated by the Salvadoran government's practice of pressing peasants into military service. Many ESAF troops were youngsters forced into service by a government desperate for military manpower. The FMLN found such unwilling, unhappy ESAF troops to be fertile ground for its recruitment efforts. Armed with insider information, the FMLN was thus able to mount effective attacks against the camp. A number of collaborators were reportedly discovered among 4th IB troopers in the months before Greg's death.

The majority of ESAF troops, however, were loyal. They called their new Green Beret trainer Sergento Rojo, Sergeant Red, because Greg's flaming red hair contrasted so sharply with his pale skin. His hair was almost orange. Celinda laughs when telling the story about Greg dressing up as a clown for a kids party in Panama—his hair was so naturally suited to a clown costume that Greg didn't even bother to don a wig.

Sergento Rojo proved to be a popular instructor. His ESAF troops liked his energy and his enthusiasm, and they liked his confidence in their abilities. He proved to be popular outside the camp as well. Part of Greg's duties were to provide humanitarian assistance to villagers who lived nearby. He identified medical needs within the village of El Paraiso and channeled medicine to the children. Sergento Rojo was a father, and he had an affinity for the kids.

Greg happened to be the only American trainer in the camp on March 31, 1987. One Green Beret assigned to the 4th IB had returned to Panama for the birth of a child, and the third Green Beret was on leave in San Salvador. Most of the ESAF troops assigned to the 4th IB were also absent from the camp that night, having deployed to various locations on assignment.

At approximately two o'clock on the morning of March 31, 1987, three FMLN Special Forces sapper units threaded their way through the minefields around the camp and penetrated the fence line at the perimeter of the camp's defenses. Perhaps with help from collaborators inside the camp, the sappers and their accompanying security teams quietly dispatched ESAF sentries and entered the interior of the compound unopposed and undetected. Greg Fronius and the remaining ESAF troops slept soundly in their bunks.

FMLN sapper units were well trained. A typical unit was comprised of ten to fifteen men. Some were sappers, specialists in explosive ordnance; the others provided covering fire as the sappers placed their explosive charges. Vietnamese military experts provided their training in camps supported by the Nicaraguans and Cubans.

The sappers in these three units carried eight-hundred-gram explosive satchels meant for use against personnel, not the buildings and structures of the camp. Their black-clad security forces were armed with H&K MP-5 automatic 9-mm machine guns, weapons favored today by police SWAT and antiterrorist teams throughout the world. In 1987, they were at the cutting edge of small-arms technology.

A fourth guerrilla unit slipped into the camp and established a firebase on a hill overlooking the encampment. Greg and his ESAF compatriots slept on. The guerrillas had achieved total surprise. They placed mortars inside their firebase and zeroed them in on preselected targets.

And then all hell broke loose. It began with a mortar barrage that poured exceptionally accurate fire on the compound without interruption for more than two hours. Buildings housing the command section, administrative offices, and troop barracks were bombarded. Sappers lobbed their charges into officers' quarters and the barracks. Chaos and confusion reigned as the guerrillas methodically destroyed the camp and killed or maimed its occupants. Accounts of Greg Fronius' actions during the FMLN assault vary in some particulars. Pandemonium reigned, and the scattered defenders caught only glimpses of him in the darkness. But eyewitness accounts agree that his determined defense of the camp was heroic and inspiring.

Awakened by the din, Greg grabbed his weapon and gear and exited his quarters. According to one account, Greg was hit in the shoulder by a bullet as soon as he stepped outside; the impact knocked him into a nearby ditch, where he applied a battle dressing to the wound.

The last thing that most people would even think to do after receiving such a wound is to rejoin the battle. Better to hunker down and wait for help. Greg moved to engage with the enemy.

As he crossed the compound, he attempted to rally ESAF troops to stage a defense of the camp. But panic reigned, and that effort failed. He then entered the courtyard surrounding the 4th IB's Tactical Operations Center (TOC). The TOC was the nerve center of the camp, the point from which a centralized defense could be conducted and from which communications to summon a rescue by ESAF forces around the country would emanate. The TOC was so central to the survival of the 4th IB that it was housed in a specially constructed bunker that was designed to withstand a determined enemy assault for at least thirty minutes—enough time to summon help.

Greg Fronius was intimately familiar with the TOC. He knew it offered a safe haven from the murderous environment in which he stood. Inside of the TOC were many of the ESAF officers who remained in the camp. He would have been welcome to join them. A prudent man would have done so until help arrived.

But Greg Fronius did not go inside the TOC. We don't know the circumstances that influenced him, but Greg clearly made a conscious decision to bypass the safety of the TOC to accomplish something he considered a higher priority than his own safety.

Across from the entrance to the TOC, and forming one side of the courtyard, was a berm—a piece of high ground. Any fighter standing on top of that berm had the tactical advantage of a direct line of fire toward the TOC. One armed with rocket-propelled grenades or a recoilless rifle, for example, could launch a direct assault against the TOC's vault door. As an expert in small unit tactics, Greg must have instantly recognized the danger a small force of guerrilla fighters on the berm would pose to the TOC. In fact, guerrillas had already occupied the berm. One explanation for Greg's next action was that he decided to defend the TOC by seizing the high ground of the berm or by sweeping the guerrilla force from it.

Alternatively, Greg may have bypassed the proffered safety of the TOC because he was committed to joining the ESAF's Special Forces in defense of the camp. This theory holds that Greg had made a pact with his counterparts to join forces in the event of an FMLN attack—or that Greg simply decided to cross the encampment to join them to defend the camp. If so, he would have run pell-mell past the TOC and over the berm en route to the Special Forces barracks.

Whatever his intentions, Greg Fronius never made it. Eyewitnesses reported he climbed a staircase from the courtyard to the top of the berm. As he approached the top step, two guerrillas confronted Greg and engaged him in a firefight at close quarters. A third guerrilla soon joined his comrades. Greg killed one of his attackers and probably wounded a second before the impact of guerrilla bullets knocked him back down the stairs.

Greg lay at the bottom of the staircase, grievously wounded. Lacking cover of any type, he was exposed to additional guerrilla fire. Two ESAF troopers at the edge of the courtyard tried to go to his aid. Greg saw them and waved them away. The risk of enemy fire was too great.

During the battle, the air burst from an enemy mortar round sprayed shrapnel down on Greg where he lay. The concussion from the explosion and the shrapnel, combined with his existing wounds, completely incapacitated him. According to one witness' account, the FMLN sappers later detonated an explosive charge under his body in retaliation for his having killed one of their comrades.

About three hours after it began its assault against El Paraiso, the FMLN force disengaged, melting away into the coming dawn. It left behind a scene of near-total destruction and death. Greg Fronius lay dead. Of the ESAF inhabitants of the encampment, nearly half were killed or wounded. For their part, the FMLN suffered only eight dead. It was a decisive victory for the rebel forces.

For his courageous actions on March 31, 1987, Greg Fronius posthumously received the Silver Star.

The attack had been so meticulously planned and so flawlessly executed that military experts almost immediately attributed its success to Nicaraguan and Cuban assistance. The rebels could not have done it alone. Some believed that the attack had actually been planned in Nicaragua or Cuba. An FMLN commander who participated in the attack later acknowledged that he had received special training in Cuba in the use of mortars.

Then there were the reports of collaborators among the ESAF troops themselves. How else could one account for the ease with which the attackers circumvented the mine fields and other defenses, the ease with which they dispatched the sentries, and the accuracy of their mortar fire? Could it have been purely coincidental that the attack occurred when the vast majority of ESAF forces were absent on field assignments, leaving the camp in a weakened if not defenseless position? It all pointed to the use of spies.

We now know that another spy was in the picture—a Cuban agent who had been at El Paraiso just weeks before, who had detailed knowledge of the camp's defense posture and the planned ESAF operations that would leave it nearly defenseless, and who had received briefings on the camp's security measures. Ana Montes had visited the camp weeks before the attack commenced.

In 1987, of course, Ana was not yet the DIA's principal Cuba analyst. She was still the agency's El Salvador and Nicaragua analyst, an expert on the military capabilities of both countries, with detailed and extensive knowledge of their militaries. As the United States increased its assistance to El Salvador during the 1980s, its insights into the Salvadoran military grew proportionately.

Ana knew every nut and bolt in the Salvadoran inventory, every bean and bullet, and many of their plans. It was her job. She was aware of the existence and mission of U.S. Special Forces on the ground and she read their after-action reports and sometimes participated in their predeployment briefings. Ana was intimately familiar with their operations.

In February and March 1987, Ana Montes took an official U.S. government-sponsored trip to El Salvador. She was in-country for five weeks. That is a long time to spend in a small country. One could almost walk around the perimeter in that period. But Ana didn't do that. Instead, her mission in El Salvador was to acquire some sense of the "ground truth" in the country to augment what she already knew. She met with a variety of U.S. military members and government employees at the embassy and made site visits to ESAF facilities throughout the country. One of her stops was in El Paraiso, where she undoubtedly received briefings on the security posture of the country's showpiece encampment and on planned operations to keep the

FMLN off balance in the region. I have no reason to believe that she and Greg Fronius ever met.

Ana was an active Cuban spy in 1987, regularly meeting with her Cuban handlers in Washington to provide information that she gleaned from work. There is no indication that Ana met with Cuban intelligence officers during her trip to El Salvador, but she certainly met with them upon her return home. And Ana got back to Washington just weeks before the attack by FMLN forces.

Did she provide actionable intelligence to her Cuban handlers about the security situation at El Paraiso? We don't know. Only Ana and her handlers know the answer to that question.

I do not blame Ana Montes for the death of Greg Fronius. To begin with, I don't know for a certainty that any information she might have provided to her Cuban handlers supported the planning for the attack against El Paraiso. We will likely never know if it did. Chances are, the attack on the compound at El Paraiso would have taken place regardless of any input Ana Montes might have provided. It seems likely that rebel forces received a sufficient amount of intelligence from collaborators and other sources to plan and execute a flawless attack with or without her. That means Greg would have died a hero's death regardless of Ana's betrayal.

As I wrote at the beginning of this chapter, for me, that's not the point. At a time when Greg Fronius depended upon her and others like her for support, Ana Montes was standing firmly in the Cuban camp. Through her chosen role as a Cuban agent, she stood opposed to everything that Greg was trying to accomplish. She stabbed him in the back.

The simple fact is this: The trusted DIA analyst who had just visited Greg's compound, the quietly dressed, professional woman who listened so attentively to all the briefings, was working for the other side. For that reason alone, whatever use the Cubans made of any subsequent trip report, I believe that Ana Montes betrayed Greg Fronius when he needed her most.

EPILOGUE

SHORTLY AFTER ANA MONTES' ARREST, I was invited to say a few words about the Montes investigation to a body of senior counterintelligence investigators representing various elements of the Department of Defense and other members of the intelligence community. My comments focused upon the ease with which the Cuban Intelligence Service had managed to penetrate DIA with their agent. They had only to meet her, recruit her, and encourage her to seek employment with my agency. Ana did the rest.

The point of my remarks was this: If it was so easy for the Cuban Intelligence Service to plant Ana Montes inside my agency, then we must assume that the Cuban Intelligence Service did it again, in other agencies as well. Cuban intelligence officers would be derelict in their duties if they failed to do so. Ana was undoubtedly skilled, bright, and dedicated. But she is far from the only intelligence professional in Washington with those attributes. She was indeed a super spy, but that's no reason to believe there aren't plenty of Cuban agents still operating at a similarly high level.

I concluded that the Cuban Intelligence Service had the capability to penetrate the U.S. government as thoroughly as the former Stasi, the East German intelligence service, had penetrated the West German government and its intelligence services during the Cold War. I assume the Cubans have done so. We have to do something about it.

My remarks were received with some interest but little action.

It was my hope that the Defense Department counterintelligence community, at least, would be motivated by the Ana Montes case to launch a full-time, dedicated, and focused effort to search for Cuban agents within the department. I met again with a subset of the original group to discuss my experience with Montes and the insights into Cuban Intelligence that I had gained from that experience. Again, my goal was to stimulate interest in launching a serious, concerted effort to search for additional Cuban agents who may be at work today inside the Department of Defense.

Once again my remarks were received with some interest and appreciation. The group made an effort on a part-time basis to conduct a broad search for Cuban agents within the Defense Department. But none of my counterparts, I am afraid, exhibited a level of motivation to finding Cuban spies within our defense establishment equal to the level of motivation exhibited by Ana Montes as she conducted espionage against us.

There seemed to be no sense of urgency within my community about detecting and countering the effects of Cuban penetrations of the U.S. government. It's as though my peers viewed Ana Montes as an anomaly, an exception rather than the rule—as though the Cubans just got lucky with Ana Montes.

I disagree. I suspect that Montes was the rule. The true exceptions may be the hot-dog vendors, the lawn caretakers, and the other low-level agents whom the Cubans may employ inside or outside of our military bases to watch the comings and goings of military aircraft, U.S. Army divisions, and U.S. Navy ships. My fear is that Cuban Intelligence is so good at their trade, they've recruited many Ana Monteses among us and planted those agents wherever they deem necessary within the U.S. government to advance their interests. It was easy for them to recruit Ana Montes. How can we deny the likelihood that they've recruited many others within the intelligence establishment?

Ana Montes was on a crusade. If we are to detect the additional Cuban agents I assume are among us, then we must go after them with equal zeal and determination, and with an almost fanatical sense of purpose. That focus and drive seems to be lacking.

Which brings me to this book. I originally wrote it to purge myself of the frustration I felt in dealing with my peers within the DoD counterintelligence community on this issue. They needed, I thought, to better understand the nature and extent of the threat posed to the United States' security by the efforts of the Cuban Intelligence Service to recruit and run spies among us. Cuba employs a very capable body of intelligence professionals who could be bleeding us dry and selling us out to our many adversaries around the world. There's no rule, as some seem to think, that information that comes to Cuba stays in Cuba. The information that the Cubans glean can be used against us; leaks to the

Cubans can cost American lives. This is a serious business, and it requires a serious response.

I essentially abandoned my effort to light a fire under my peers and opted instead to publish this book. The media coverage of the Ana Montes case was woefully inadequate. It failed to capture the exceptionally grave damage to national security that was inflicted by just one motivated woman. Few in the media seemed to care, and as a result, the public simply did not "get it." I hope this book will in some small way set the record straight and, in the process, increase public awareness of the threat posed to our way of life by the Cuban Intelligence Service and the agents they've almost certainly placed among us.

I will receive no compensation for this work. It's not about money. I waived my copyright and released this manuscript without conditions to an acquaintance in the publishing business who seemed to understand and appreciate my frustration with the system in which I work. He arranged to funnel the proceeds from the sale of this book to the children of Greg Fronius, who gave his life to advance the interests of the United States. I think that's appropriate. Ana Montes may or may not have been responsible for the deaths of American fighting men and women through her espionage, but in a rather ironic twist, her story will assist the family of one such warfighter in another fashion. I like that.

Steve McCoy has retired from the FBI and is now pursuing private interests. Pete continues to serve us as a special agent of the FBI; he is good at his job, and the American people can expect to reap the benefit of his accomplishments in the future. Steve, Pete, and their many colleagues at the FBI who conducted and supported the investigation of Ana Montes deserve our respect and heartfelt thanks. These are good people. I wish the media would stop bashing their organization.

Chris Simmons and John Kavanagh continue to serve as counterintelligence analysts for DIA. We forged a bond through our experience on the Ana Montes investigation that promises an interesting and productive future for us as we continue to work together in the world of counterintelligence. Never in my experience had investigators and analysts worked so closely or productively with one another as we did during the year that we focused our combined efforts on Havana Ana. May our experience serve as a model for future investigations and operations.

Reg Brown also remains at DIA and, from what I gather, has no immediate plans for other employment. That's good. He talks occasionally about shucking the intelligence business altogether and earning a living from his pastime, making pottery, but I hope he's not serious. You make beautiful pottery, Reg, but I need you where you are. To my knowledge, never before in the history of U.S. counterintelligence was a spy identified and eventually brought to justice through the application of analytic methods. Reg did that. I want him to stay around to point me in the right direction again.

Bobby Speegle is close to retirement age but remains at the time of this writing at DIA, serving us all. Thanks, Bobby. You were great. You deserve an Oscar.

Dave Curtin accepted an offer to work for another agency of the federal government that is directly involved in the war on terrorism. Dave, I stand in awe of you. You always came through for me when I needed you most. You required so little direction, and you really know how to get things done. The American people are fortunate that you've chosen to serve us in your current capacity.

Gator speaks incessantly about seeking employment elsewhere, but I think it's just talk. He loves this line of work, and we have a lot of fun together at DIA. We share a common view of our world. But remember, Gator: You can't expect to find a spy under every rock or behind every tree. You simply have to believe that a spy is there, somewhere, and that if you look under every rock and behind every tree, you will eventually find him. I expect Gator to remain welded to my hip for another decade or so.

Ana Montes will serve her time productively, I am sure. Knowing Ana, she'll be running the place before too long. I understand that she remains unrepentant about providing information to the Cubans. She still believes that she did the right, just, and moral thing in supporting them, and I suspect that she will hold that view for the rest of her life. That's fine. At least she's no longer in a position to cause the rest of us any harm. Ana Montes is now incarcerated near Fort Worth, Texas.

Ana's boyfriend, Bill, has had a rough time of it. He requested and received permission to remain in contact with Ana after her arrest, up until she was convicted. He sensed, understandably, that she needed his support during an emotional time in her life. But he made clear to me, during one of several meetings on the subject, that his support for Ana would end if and when she was convicted of the crime. Bill was as good as his word. Part of him feels sorry for Ana, but he can never understand or condone what she did. He is torn, but Bill is moving forward with his life without her.

As for me, I continue to march. There are some among my peers in this business who take exception to my having published a book about my experience on the job. It goes against their grain. Some may even avoid working with me in the future, for fear that their actions and words will end up in a book somewhere or because they feel that I've crossed an ethical line by publishing this story. I understand. So be it.

I remain firmly focused on my mission. I am not a writer. I am a counter-intelligence investigator. And my job is to detect and investigate espionage and suspected espionage within the Defense Intelligence Agency. I've performed that job for almost two decades now, and I expect to continue performing it until my youngest son, now ten, graduates from high school. I'm not going away.

The readers of this book will undoubtedly include members of the Cuban Intelligence Service and the other agents whom they've placed among us. To the Cuban service, I doff my hat. Well done. I hope that more than one of you was fired, however, when you lost Ana Montes as your agent. As for the spies among us, those who still work for Cuban Intelligence: Watch your back. You may soon find me or one of my compatriots from the FBI standing behind you, ready to put the cuffs on.

INDEX

ABOUT THE AUTHOR

SCOTT W. CARMICHAEL serves as the senior security and counterintelligence investigator for the Defense Intelligence Agency (DIA) and served as the lead case agent for the DIA on the Ana B. Montes espionage investigation. He has accumulated a total of twenty-six years of federal service, including a four-year tour as a Chinese-Mandarin linguist in the U.S. Navy, employment as a special agent of the Naval Criminal Investigative Service (NCIS), and more than eighteen years as a counterintelligence investigator for the DIA. His awards include the National Intelligence Medal of Achievement, the National Intelligence Meritorious Unit Award, two DIA Director's Awards, numerous Letters of Appreciation from the director of the FBI, and many lesser forms of recognition for contributions toward the successful resolution of a variety of national security matters. He lives with his wife and three sons in the Washington, D.C., metropolitan area.

ſ